8/13

O9-BUC-525

Last-Minute

KITCHEN

SECRETS

DISCARD

JOEY GREEN

128 INGENIOUS TIPS

TO SURVIVE LUMPY GRAVY,
WILTED LETTUCE, CRUMBLING CAKE,
AND OTHER COOKING DISASTERS

CHICAGO
REVIEW
PRESS

Copyright © 2018 by Joey Green

All rights reserved. No part of this book may be reproduced in any form or by any electronic or mechanical means, including information storage and retrieval systems, without the written permission of the publisher.

A responsible adult should supervise any young reader who conducts the kitchen secrets in this book to avoid potential dangers and injuries. The author has conducted every kitchen secret in this book and has made every reasonable effort to ensure that the kitchen secrets are safe when conducted as instructed. However, neither the author nor the publisher assumes any liability for damages caused or injury sustained from conducting the kitchen secrets in this book.

Published by Chicago Review Press Incorporated
814 North Franklin Street
Chicago, Illinois 60610
ISBN 978-0-912777-58-0

Library of Congress Cataloging-in-Publication Data
Names: Green, Joey, author.
Title: Last-minute kitchen secrets : 128 ingenious tips to survive lumpy
  gravy, wilted lettuce, crumbling cake, and other cooking disasters / Joey
  Green.
Description: Chicago, Illinois : Chicago Review Press, [2018] | Includes
  bibliographical references.
Identifiers: LCCN 2017051837 (print) | LCCN 2017055906 (ebook) | ISBN
  9780912777597 (adobe pdf) | ISBN 9780912777603 (kindle) | ISBN
  9780912777610 (epub) | ISBN 9780912777580 (trade paper)
Subjects: LCSH: Cooking—Miscellanea. | Quick and easy cooking—Miscellanea.
Classification: LCC TX651 (ebook) | LCC TX651 .G74 2018 (print) | DDC
  641.5—dc23
LC record available at https://lccn.loc.gov/2017051837

Cover and interior design: Andrew Brozyna, AJB Design Inc.
Cover and interior layout: Jonathan Hahn
Cover and interior photos: Julia Green, Joey Green, and Debbie Green

Printed in the United States of America
5 4 3 2 1

CONTENTS

9 KITCHEN AND FOLK REMEDIES 189

10 CLEANING TRICKS 207

Introduction

Imagine the situation. You've invited family and friends over to your place for dinner. You're slaving away in the kitchen. You've timed everything perfectly. As you're setting the table, you suddenly smell something burning. You race back into the kitchen. Smoke rises from a saucepan on the stove. It's the gravy. It's no longer recognizable. How do you avert this horrid disaster? Can this meal be saved before the doorbell rings?

Cooking can be a madcap adventure, a series of exhilarating accomplishments, a nonstop banquet of incredible taste sensations. Or a cataclysmic fiasco.

We amateur chefs face a never-ending flood of seemingly insurmountable and unpredictable setbacks. A cut of beef shrinks to the size of a hockey puck. The mashed potatoes turn soggy and taste like wallpaper paste. A pot of overcooked beans morphs into sludge. A freshly baked cake gets hopelessly stuck in the pan, crumbling into chunks when you attempt to remove it. Baked-on food permanently bonds to a casserole dish. The refrigerator reeks of sour milk. And the sink is clogged.

Most kitchen mishaps seem catastrophic and overwhelming, but like John Lennon said, "There are no problems, only solutions." It's just a matter of perspective. If you're willing to think outside the breadbox and embrace your inner master chef, you'll discover ingenious solutions staring you straight in the face. You don't have to hurl those mushy vegetables in the trash, run out to the grocery store to buy a box of Hot Pockets, or scrap your plans and head for the nearest restaurant. You have several products in your kitchen right now that you can use to save the soufflé.

Don't have a rolling pin? Use an aluminum baseball bat. Stubborn jar lid? Warm it with a blow-dryer. No cream cheese? Substitute yogurt. Need a salad spinner? Use a pillowcase. All out of sugar? Try pancake syrup. Onions bringing you to tears? Put on a swimming mask.

Preventing and salvaging any cooking disasters is as easy as pie, provided you know a few last-minute kitchen secrets to avoid burning the crust of that pie. In these pages, you'll learn how to speed up a baked potato with a carpenter's nail. You'll discover how to bread chicken croquettes with potato chips, how to strain fat from soup with lettuce, and how to make dough rise with a heating pad. You'll find out how to cover up a cracked cheesecake with sour cream, stop a baking pie from boiling over with pasta, and poach a fish with panty hose. Plus you'll learn how to cook a salmon in a dishwasher, shrimp in the clothes dryer, and ramen noodles in a coffeemaker.

I hope this book gives you plenty of simple tricks, clever shortcuts, and innovative hacks to turn your cooking disasters into delightful surprises.

If not, you can always use this book as a meat mallet.

Bon appétit!

1

SHOPPING AND STORAGE

While getting ready to leave on a two-week vacation, I noticed an open jar of mayonnaise in the refrigerator. Afraid the mayonnaise wouldn't keep while we were gone, I placed the jar in the freezer.

When we returned home, my wife, Debbie, opened the freezer to find the mayonnaise jar filled with large white chunks floating in yellow oil. "What did you do?" she asked, holding up the jar.

"I can fix it," I promised. I placed the jar on the countertop and let it thaw to room temperature. Then I shook the jar for a good five minutes to mix the emulsion back together.

But no matter how hard I shook that jar, the mayonnaise remained chunks of white curd in yellow oil. I even ran the mixture through the blender—but to no avail. When Debbie left the house, I secretly drove to the grocery store, bought another jar of mayonnaise, and placed it in the refrigerator.

"See," I told Debbie when she got home, holding up the jar. "Good as new."

"Nice try," she said. "I saw you at the grocery store."

How to Prevent Apples from Going Bad with a Hole Puncher

WHAT YOU NEED

- Hole puncher
- Resealable plastic bag, gallon size
- Fresh apples

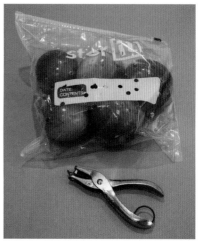

WHAT TO DO

1. Using a hole puncher, perforate a few holes in the resealable plastic bag.
2. Place the apples inside the plastic bag and seal the bag shut.
3. Store in the refrigerator or fruit bin.
4. If you see any apples going bad, remove the rotten apples from the bag before they contaminate the good fruit.

HOW IT WORKS

One bad apple really can spoil the whole bunch. The excessive ethylene gas produced by the bad apple triggers the healthy apples to rot. The holes in the plastic bag permit air movement while allowing the bag to retain the ethylene that hastens ripening.

HOW ABOUT THEM APPLES?

- If you don't have a plastic bag, store apples in the fruit bin in your refrigerator, but make sure they do not touch each other—to prevent bad apples from spoiling good apples.
- Apples retain their freshness for at least two weeks and sometimes up to one month.
- Rehydrate dried-out apples by cutting them into slices and soaking the pieces in a bowl of apple cider.

How to Revive Hardened Brown Sugar with a Slice of Bread

WHAT YOU NEED

- Airtight plastic container (or a resealable plastic bag)
- 1 or 2 slices of fresh white bread (or several marshmallows)

WHAT TO DO

1. To revive a box of hardened brown sugar, empty the brown sugar into an airtight container or resealable plastic bag.
2. Place one or two slices of white bread (or several marshmallows) on top of the brown sugar.
3. Seal the lid on the container.
4. Let sit undisturbed for one or two days.
5. When the brown sugar becomes soft again, discard the bread.

HOW IT WORKS

Brown sugar hardens due to loss of moisture. The bread gives off water vapor, returning the moisture to the brown sugar and softening it.

SOFTEN UP

- Brown sugar is sugar coated with a thin coat of molasses, the thick brown syrup obtained from raw sugar during the refining process. Exposure to air causes molasses to lose moisture and harden. Rehydrating the hardened molasses softens it.
- Heating brown sugar in a microwave for 30 seconds does soften the molasses, but only temporarily. The molasses hardens again within a couple of minutes.
- Don't have any white bread? Pour the brown sugar into an airtight container, cover it with a sheet of plastic wrap, place a damp paper towel on top of the plastic wrap, and seal the lid securely. Let sit for one or two days.

- Storing brown sugar inside a sealed plastic bag or an airtight container kept in the freezer prevents the brown sugar from hardening—as does placing a few marshmallows in the bag, box, or jar of sugar.
- For another way to unclump hardened brown sugar, empty the brown sugar into a plastic airtight container, place a couple of marshmallows on top of the sugar, seal the lid securely, and let sit for two or three days.

EVERY TRICK IN THE BOOK

A Spoonful of Sugar

You can also use brown sugar to:

- **Add a Butterscotch Flavor to Brownies.** Substitute brown sugar for the white sugar in the recipe.
- **Bake a Cake in a Jell-O Mold.** Grease and flour the mold thoroughly and then sprinkle the bottom of the mold well with brown sugar before pouring in the batter. The detailed design on the bottom of the mold will be transferred to the top of the cake, glazed with brown sugar.
- **Make Pancake Syrup.** If you're all out of maple syrup, mix 1 cup of brown sugar and ½ cup of water in a saucepan, bring to a boil, and let simmer for 15 minutes. Add 1 teaspoon of imitation maple flavor or vanilla extract to suit your taste.

How to Keep Cheese Fresh with Sugar Cubes

WHAT YOU NEED
- Block of cheese
- Sugar cubes
- Resealable plastic bag

WHAT TO DO
1. To prevent mold from forming on a block of cheese, place the cheese and a few sugar cubes in a resealable plastic bag.
2. Seal the bag partially shut.
3. Suck out the excess air from the bag, and seal tightly.
4. Change the sugar cubes every few days.

HOW IT WORKS
The sugar cubes attract the mold spores away from the cheese.

SAY CHEESE
- To prevent a block of cheese from getting mwoldy, dampen a piece of cheesecloth with apple cider vinegar, and wrap it around the block of cheese. Place the wrapped block of cheese in a resealable plastic bag or airtight container, and refrigerate. The acetic acid in the vinegar helps prevent the growth of mold and does not alter the flavor of the cheese. When necessary, add more vinegar to the cheesecloth.
- Another way to prevent cheese from growing mold in the refrigerator: Dissolve 2 tablespoons of salt in 3 cups of water, dampen a cloth with the salt water, and wrap the block of cheese in the damp cloth. Place the wrapped cheese in a resealable plastic bag or airtight container and refrigerate.
- Natural cheese contains vital enzymes and bacteria that need air and moisture to survive. To create a healthy microenvironment for the enzymes and bacteria to thrive, rewrap a block of cheese in a sheet of waxed paper, followed by a sheet of plastic wrap, and refrigerate. After using a portion of the cheese, rewrap the remaining block in fresh waxed paper and fresh plastic wrap.
- To prevent mold from forming on grated cheese, place the grated cheese in a resealable plastic bag, seal the bag partially shut, suck out the excess air from the bag, and seal tightly. Store the bag in the freezer.
- The following cheeses can be frozen and will remain fresh when thawed: cheddar, French, Greek, Italian, Swiss, and processed cheese.

WHEN DO WE EAT?

How to Choose and Store Cheese

BUYING:

- Check the aroma, appearance, and flavor of any cheese you wish to buy. Never buy any cheese that smells like ammonia, sour milk, or a barnyard. Avoid cheese that appears cracked, discolored, or moldy (except for blue cheese). And before buying the cheese, try to taste a sample.
- Do not buy more cheese than you will eat within a few days.

STORING:

- Keep cheese in the refrigerator's vegetable or fruit bin (where the humidity is highest), with the temperature set between 35° and 45° Fahrenheit.
- Place strong, pungent cheeses in airtight containers to prevent the bouquet from suffusing other foods in your refrigerator.
- Separate different types of cheeses from each other in the refrigerator to prevent them from acquiring the others' flavor.
- Store containers of cottage cheese or ricotta cheese upside down in the refrigerator to prolong their shelf life.
- Store blue cheese and Roquefort cheese in the freezer. To prepare a salad, use a paring knife to scrape the cheese, causing it to crumble beautifully.

SAFEGUARDING:

- If blue-green mold develops on the skin of hard cheeses (excluding fresh cheese or blue cheese), use a paring knife to cut it off approximately ½ inch below the surface of the mold. The remaining cheese is safe to eat.
- If any cheese becomes excessively dry, develops a slimy texture, or smells like a hint of ammonia or any other strange odor, throw it away.
- Grate hard cheeses like cheddar, Parmesan, and Romano before melting them for better results.

How to Store Egg Yolks with Salt

WHAT YOU NEED
- Measuring spoons
- ⅛ teaspoon of salt
- ½ cup of cool water
- Clean, empty jar
- Egg yolks with unbroken membranes
- Refrigerator

WHAT TO DO
1. To store unbroken egg yolks intact for up to one week, dissolve ⅛ teaspoon of salt into ½ cup of cool water.
2. Pour the salty solution into a jar.
3. Carefully slide the yolk into the jar without breaking the membrane, making certain the salt water covers the yolk completely.
4. Seal the lid and refrigerate.
5. Before using the yolk, simply drain the salt water.

HOW IT WORKS
The salt water prevents the egg yolks from congealing.

A HARD EGG TO CRACK
- To freeze beaten egg yolks, blend in a pinch of sugar, pour the mixture into an airtight container, cover, and freeze. The sugar prevents the yolks from coagulating.
- To make an eggbeater easy to clean, spray the beaters with cooking spray before beating eggs so sticky foods wash off effortlessly.
- If you run out of eggs while baking a cake, substitute 1 teaspoon of baking soda and 1 teaspoon of white vinegar for each egg.
- If you run out of eggs when cooking anything other than cake, substitute 1 teaspoon of cornstarch for each egg.

How to Detect Fresh Eggs with a Glass of Water

WHAT YOU NEED
- A glass of water

WHAT TO DO
1. To determine whether an egg is fresh, gently lower the egg into a glass of water.
2. If the egg sinks to the bottom of the glass and lies on its side, the egg is fresh. If the egg sinks the bottom but stands upright, use the egg as soon as possible. If the egg floats, it has gone bad.

HOW IT WORKS

Eggshells are porous, meaning air passes through tiny holes in the shell. Over time, as more air passes into the egg, the liquid inside the egg begins to evaporate. The whites thin out, and the yolks flatten. The older the egg, the more air inside the shell and the more buoyant the egg.

WALKING ON EGGS
- If you can't place the egg in a glass of water, crack open the egg into a bowl and smell it. A fresh egg will have no odor. A bad egg smells like sulfur.
- Fresh eggs can be stored in their original carton for up to five weeks in the refrigerator.
- Hard-boiled eggs can be stored in their shell in the refrigerator for 8 to 10 days.
- Don't buy cracked eggs. While in the store, open the carton and make sure no eggs have cracked. Bacteria can enter the egg through cracks in the shell. If purchased eggs crack on the way home from the grocery store, break them into a clean, airtight container, cover it securely, place it in the refrigerator, and use the eggs within two days. Cook the broken eggs thoroughly (until the whites and yolks coagulate) to kill any bacteria.

How to Keep Herbs with an Ice Cube Tray

WHAT YOU NEED
- Fresh herbs
- Water
- Sharp kitchen knife
- Cutting board
- Ice cube tray
- Freezer
- Teaspoon
- Wine
- Resealable freezer bag
- Indelible marker

WHAT TO DO
1. Rinse the herbs with water.
2. Using a sharp kitchen knife and a cutting board, carefully slice the herbs into small pieces.
3. Fill each compartment in an ice cube tray with 1 teaspoon of cut fresh herbs.
4. Fill the rest of each compartment with wine.
5. Place the ice cube tray in the freezer.
6. After the herb-filled ice cubes freeze solid, pop the cubes from the tray, and place them in a resealable freezer bag.
7. Using an indelible marker, label the bag with name of the herb.
8. Store the herb cubes in the freezer.
9. Whenever a recipe calls for 1 teaspoon of that herb, place one ice cube in the mixing bowl or saucepan.

HOW IT WORKS
Freezing the herbs inside a block of frozen wine keeps the herbs fresh. The alcohol in the wine helps preserve the herb and evaporates when heated in a saucepan.

BREAKING THE ICE
- Prevent ice cube trays from sticking to the floor of the freezer by placing a sheet of waxed paper under the trays (or any container you store in the freezer).
- To dry fresh herbs, place the herbs on a paper towel and heat them in the microwave oven for approximately 1 minute. Repeat for 30-second

intervals if needed. Pour the dried herbs into resealable plastic bags (being sure to suck out the air), label the bags with an indelible marker, and store in the pantry for up to one year.

- Stored in an airtight container in a cool, dry place, whole spices retain their potency for up to four years, ground spices last two to three years, and leafy herbs keep their flavor for one to three years.

- To make fresh onion salt, cut off the top of an onion, sprinkle salt over the open slice, and let sit for a few minutes. The salt absorbs the onion juice. Scrape off the salt with a knife, and place in a small spice bowl.

- Make flavored vinegar by pouring a bottle of wine vinegar into a saucepan, adding herbs like celery, dill seeds, rosemary, or tarragon, and simmering. Let cool, pour back into the bottle, and store.

- Avoid spills when pouring spices into a shaker or a measuring spoon by working over a sheet of waxed paper. If the spices spill, fold the sheet of waxed paper in half, and pour the spice back into its bottle.

EVERY TRICK IN THE BOOK
Walking on Thin Ice

You can also use an ice cube tray to:

- **Freeze Egg Whites.** If you have leftover egg whites when baking, pour them into the compartments of an ice cube tray and freeze for your next project. Each compartment holds exactly 1 egg white. Once they freeze, pop out the cubes, and store in a plastic freezer bag until needed.

- **Make Better Iced Coffee.** Rather than diluting iced coffee with the melted water from typical ice cubes, brew a pot of coffee, pour the coffee into an ice cube tray, and freeze. Store the frozen coffee cubes in a resealable plastic bag in the freezer and use to ice iced coffee.

- **Preserve Single Servings of Pesto.** Preserve a heaping tablespoon of pesto sauce inside a single compartment of an ice cube tray, and freeze for later. Once frozen, store the pesto cube in a plastic freezer bag, and thaw when needed.

How to Prevent Jars from Dripping with Margarine Lids

WHAT YOU NEED

- Clean plastic lids from margarine tubs (or coffee cans)

WHAT TO DO

1. To avoid cleaning oil drips from pantry shelves and countertops, use clean plastic lids from used margarine tubs or coffee cans as coasters for storing bottles of oil, honey, and salad dressing in the pantry.
2. Plastic lids can also be used as coasters to place bottles of oil or other ingredients on the countertop when cooking.
3. When the plastic lid becomes too sticky, wash the used plastic lid with soapy water made with dishwashing liquid and reuse.

HOW IT WORKS

When placed upside down on a flat surface, the plastic lid from a margarine tub or coffee can, with its raised edge, serves as a small saucer.

PUT A LID ON IT

Used as coasters for cans in the pantry, plastic lids also prevent cans of food from leaving rust rings on shelves.

EVERY TRICK IN THE BOOK
Flip Your Lid

You can also use a plastic lid to:

- **Rest a Cooking Spoon.** A plastic lid makes an excellent spoon rest when cooking.
- **Catch Popsicle Drips.** Using a knife or a pair of sharp scissors, carefully cut an X or two in a plastic lid and insert the sticks of a Popsicle to catch any drips. Afterward, wash for reuse.
- **Separate Homemade Hamburger Patties.** Place a clean plastic lid between each patty before freezing to make separating the patties later a snap.

How to Store Plastic Grocery Bags in a Tissue Box

WHAT YOU NEED

- Clean, empty tissue box (or plastic box)

WHAT TO DO

1. Insert the bottom of a plastic grocery into the slot in the top of the tissue box and continue stuffing the bag into the box, leaving the handle exposed through the slot.

2. Insert the bottom of a second plastic grocery bag through the handle of the first bag, and continue stuffing the two bags into the box, leaving the handle of the second bag exposed through the slot.

3. Continue the process with all the plastic grocery bags you have, leaving the handle of the last bag sticking up from the slot in the tissue box.

4. When you need a plastic bag, simply pull the exposed handle like a tissue, removing one bag from the box. The handle of the next bag will automatically pop up through the slot.

HOW IT WORKS

When you tug the exposed handle, removing one plastic bag from the box, the tail end of the bag pulls the handle of the next bag through the slot in the box, the same way tissues replenish themselves in a tissue box.

How to Keep Strawberries Fresh with a Coffee Filter

WHAT YOU NEED

- Airtight plastic container
- Paper coffee filter
- Refrigerator

WHAT TO DO

1. To keep unwashed strawberries fresh, place the strawberries in an airtight plastic container.
2. Place a folded paper coffee filter on top of the strawberries.
3. Secure the lid, and store upside down in the refrigerator.

HOW IT WORKS

The coffee filter absorbs any excess moisture that might otherwise turn the strawberries soggy.

GET FRESH

- Store strawberries in a colander in the refrigerator. The cold air circulates around the strawberries, keeping them fresh for several days.
- Do not remove the stems from strawberries or slice them until after you wash them. Hulled and sliced strawberries absorb water and become soggy, losing their flavor.
- To wash strawberries quickly and efficiently, fill the sink halfway with water and toss in the strawberries. As the small red fruits float on the surface, use the spray attachment to shower the strawberries with cold water and make them tumble in the water. After the dirt, grit, and

sand sink to the bottom, pluck out the strawberries. Drain the water from the sink, and repeat the process if need be.

EVERY TRICK IN THE BOOK

Wake Up and Smell the Coffee

You can also use a coffee filter to:

- **Weigh Chopped Foods on a Kitchen Scale Without Making a Mess.** Place the chopped ingredients in a paper coffee filter and weigh them together.
- **Store Cast-Iron Pots or Pans.** Place a paper coffee filter inside the cookware. The paper filter absorbs excess moisture, preventing rust. Replace the coffee filter every time you use the pot or pan.
- **Protect Fine China Dishes.** Place a coffee filter between each plate when stacking the dishes to create a buffer.
- **Substitute for a Napkin.** If you run out of napkins, use a coffee filter in a pinch.
- **Safeguard Nonstick Pots and Pans.** Before stacking nonstick pots and pans, place a coffee filter between each one to help prevent scratches on the sensitive surface.
- **Prevent Food Spatters in the Microwave Oven.** Place a coffee filter over the cup, bowl, or plate containing the food or drink. The coffee filter will serve as a lid.
- **Separate Brownies or Cookies.** Coffee filters placed between layers of brownies or cookies on a serving plate prevent the desserts from sticking to each other.
- **Make Party Favors.** Set a handful of candy in the center of a coffee filter and tie the fanned sides together with a ribbon.
- **Strain Homemade Jelly.** Use a coffee filter as a sieve to sift any impurities.
- **Recycle Frying Oil.** Line a metal strainer with a coffee filter to clarify vegetable oil after deep-frying.
- **Strain Fat from Beef or Chicken Broth.** Place a coffee filter in the bottom of a strainer or colander, and slowly pour the broth through the paper filter to strain out the fat.
- **Hold Messy Foods.** A coffee filter, folded in half, holds a taco.

How to Prevent Moisture in Sugar with a Saltine Cracker

WHAT YOU NEED
- Resealable airtight container
- Fresh saltine crackers

WHAT TO DO
1. Pour the sugar into a resealable airtight container.
2. Place a few fresh saltine crackers inside the container of sugar.
3. Seal the lid.

HOW IT WORKS
The crackers absorb excess moisture and prevent the sugar from clumping.

EVERY TRICK IN THE BOOK
Wisecrackers

You can also use saltine crackers to:

- **Clean a Meat Grinder.** When grinded through the gadget, the crackers clean away meat scraps and absorb any residual moisture, preventing meat from sticking to the grinder.
- **Make Substitute Bread Crumbs.** Grind saltine crackers in a blender (or place in a resealable plastic bag and run over with a rolling pin), and substitute ¾ cup of cracker crumbs for every cup of bread crumbs called for by a recipe.

- **Make Meatloaf.** Grind saltine crackers in a blender (or place in a resealable plastic bag and run over them with a rolling pin), and mix ¾ cup of cracker crumbs for every 1 pound of ground beef.
- **Prevent Scalloped Potatoes from Curdling.** Instead of using flour as called for by the recipe, use roughly a dozen crushed saltine crackers to thicken scalloped potatoes.
- **Make Stuffing.** Place saltine crackers in a resealable plastic bag, run over them with a rolling pin, and fill only half the bird cavity to give the cracker crumbs ample room to swell.

How to Store Potatoes, Onions, and Garlic with Panty Hose

WHAT YOU NEED
- Scissors
- Clean, used pair of panty hose

WHAT TO DO
1. Use a pair of scissors to snip off the foot from a clean, used pair of panty hose.
2. Drop a potato, onion, or garlic clove into the foot of the leg and tie a knot above it.
3. Continue adding potatoes, onions, or garlic cloves—one at a time—and tying a knot between them.
4. Hang the filled panty hose leg from a hook on the back of a door.
5. When you need a potato, onion, or garlic clove, use a pair of scissors to simply cut one off from the bottom—just under the knot.

HOW IT WORKS
The nylon hose allows air to circulate around the potatoes, onions, or garlic cloves, keeping them fresh longer. Also, the nylon prevents rodents or insects from eating the herbs or vegetables.

MAKING THE ROUNDS
- To remove garlic skin easily and effortlessly, heat the clove in the microwave oven for 10 seconds to loosen the skin. Remove the clove and press it against the countertop.
- To substitute garlic powder for fresh garlic, use ¼ teaspoon powdered garlic for each garlic clove in the recipe.
- A pound of onions yields roughly 4 cups of sliced or chopped onion.
- Spanish (golden) onions have a sweet flavor, white onions have a soft flavor, and red (Italian) onions have a light flavor.
- A pound of potatoes yields approximately 2 cups of mashed potatoes.

- Store cut onions in a sealed glass jar—not a plastic container—in the refrigerator. Plastic containers absorb onion odor.
- Storing potatoes in a dry place in the refrigerator prevents the eyes from sprouting.
- To harden raw potatoes that have become soft, immerse them in ice water for 30 minutes.

EVERY TRICK IN THE BOOK
Smarty Pants

You can also use a panty hose to:

- **Clean the Dust Bunnies from Under a Refrigerator.** Using a pair of scissors, snip off one leg from a clean, used pair of panty hose. Insert the end of a yardstick or broomstick into the leg, slip the nylon-covered stick under the refrigerator, and slide the baton back and forth. The dust bunnies cling to the nylon hose.
- **Clean a Sticky Pancake Griddle.** Cut off the foot from a clean, used pair of panty hose, fill it with salt, and tie a knot in the end. Rub the hot griddle with the sachet of salt.
- **Rinse Salad Greens.** Stretch a clean, used pair of panty hose over the mouth of a colander and fill with salad greens. After rinsing the greens under running water, remove the panty hose with the greens still inside, and shake over the sink. Step outside, and gripping the panty hose closed, twirl over your head to remove any excess water.
- **Prolong the Usefulness of a Sponge.** Using scissors, cut off one foot from a clean pair of panty hose. Insert a brand-new sponge into the foot, and tie a knot in the open end. The nylon sachet holds the sponge together when it starts crumbling.
- **Clean Kitchen Magnets in the Dishwasher.** Cut off one foot from a clean, used pair of panty hose, place the kitchen magnets in the foot, and knot the open end. Place the sachet in the silverware bin (or tie the end to one of the racks) and put it through the regular cycle.

How to Ripen Tomatoes with Newspaper

WHAT YOU NEED

- Cardboard box or shoe box
- Newspaper
- Green tomatoes
- 1 ripening apple or banana (optional)

WHAT TO DO

1. To accelerate the ripening of tomatoes, line the inside of a cardboard box or shoebox with newspaper.
2. Place the box in a warm place indoors.
3. Place the green tomatoes inside the box on top of the newspaper in a single layer with a little space between each tomato so they do not touch each other.
4. To speed up the ripening process even further, set a ripening apple or banana inside the box (not touching any of the green tomatoes).
5. Cover the green tomatoes (and apple or banana) with a single sheet of newspaper.
6. Close the cover of the box, and let the tomatoes sit undisturbed.
7. Check the tomatoes once daily.

HOW IT WORKS

The newspaper keeps the ethylene, the natural gas produced by tomatoes that causes them to ripen, close to the fruit. The ripening apple or banana produces additional ethylene.

WHEN THE TIME IS RIPE

Other ways to ripen green tomatoes:

- Using the tines of a fork, punch a few holes in a brown paper bag. Place the green tomatoes and a ripening apple or banana in the bag. Close the bag, and set it in a dark place at room temperature for a few days. Check the tomatoes periodically, and discard any rotten or moldy ones. The holes in the bag allow air to circulate, helping to prevent mold.
- Wrap each green tomato in an individual sheet of newspaper, place them on a tray, and set in a dark room at roughly 70° Fahrenheit.
- Uproot the entire tomato plant with the tomatoes attached, bring it indoors, and let the tomatoes ripen on the vine.

EVERY TRICK IN THE BOOK

Break the News

You can also use newspaper to:

- **Keep a Watermelon Cool on the Go.** When taking a chilled watermelon on a picnic, seal in the coolness by wrapping the watermelon in newspaper, secured in place with Scotch tape.
- **Deodorize a Refrigerator or Freezer.** Empty all the food items from the appliance, unplug it, fill it with crumpled sheets of newspaper, and shut the door. Let the refrigerator sit undisturbed for several days, giving the newsprint plenty of time to absorb the putrid odors.
- **Reduce the Number of Paper Towels Needed to Absorb Fat from Bacon Strips.** Place several sections of a newspaper under a sheet of paper towel to absorb any fat that permeates the towel.
- **Thaw a Frozen Roast.** Set the roast on a cake-cooling rack, and place several sections of a newspaper on a cookie sheet positioned under the rack to catch the juices.
- **Deodorize a Plastic Container.** Stuff crumpled-up newspaper into the container, replace the lid securely, and let sit for several days to allow the newsprint to absorb the fetid odors. Remove the newspaper, and wash the revived container with soapy water, rinse clean, and dry.

How to Preserve Diced Ginger with Vodka

WHAT YOU NEED

- Scouring pad
- Fresh ginger root
- Teaspoon
- Paring knife
- Clean, empty glass jar with lid
- Vodka (or sherry)
- Refrigerator

WHAT TO DO

1. Using a scouring pad, clean the fresh ginger root by scrubbing under running water.
2. Holding a teaspoon by its handle, scrape the edge of the spoon's bowl against the ginger root, as if scraping a carrot, to remove the skin.

3. Using a paring knife, dice the fresh ginger.
4. Place the diced ginger in a jar.
5. Top off with vodka (or sherry), and secure the lid.
6. Place the jar on a shelf in your refrigerator.

HOW IT WORKS

The ginger will last up to one year in the refrigerator.

OLD SPICE

- If you don't have any vodka for the tip above, use white vinegar.
- You can also store ginger for months by simply burying the root in moist soil outdoors or in a flowerpot.
- A peeled ginger root can be preserved in the freezer for several months, and when you need some ginger, grate as much of the frozen root as you need, replacing the unused portion in the freezer.

How to Dry Mushrooms with Dental Floss

WHAT YOU NEED

- Water
- Hand towel
- Paring knife
- Cutting board
- Large needle
- Dental floss
- Airtight plastic container with lid
- Chicken stock or beef stock

WHAT TO DO

1. Wash the mushrooms quickly in water—without soaking or immerse the mushrooms in the water.
2. Immediately pat the mushrooms dry with a hand towel. Otherwise, these absorbent fungi quickly become waterlogged and tasteless.
3. Cut the mushrooms in half lengthwise with a paring knife on a cutting board.
4. Using a large needle and dental floss, string the mushrooms together, leaving 1 inch between each mushroom half.

5. Hang the string of mushrooms outdoors in sunlight for two days or until completely dry.
6. Store in an airtight container on the pantry shelf.
7. Rehydrate dried mushrooms by soaking them in water, chicken stock, or beef stock for 1 hour.

HOW IT WORKS

Hanging mushrooms outdoors in sunlight allows the heat from the sun to dehydrate the mushrooms, increasing the vitamin D content in many gilled mushroom species.

How to Vacuum Seal Food with a Bowl of Water

WHAT YOU NEED

- Resealable plastic bag
- Large mixing bowl (or pot)
- Water
- Kitchen towel
- Refrigerator or freezer

WHAT TO DO

1. Place the food item inside the resealable plastic bag.
2. Seal the bag, leaving a 1-inch opening at one side.
3. Holding the bag upright by its top, lower the bag into a large mixing bowl or pot filled with water.
4. Lower the entire bag (except for the open top) into the water, which will remove all the air from the bag.
5. Seal the bag securely shut.
6. Remove the bag from the water, dry with a towel, and refrigerate or freeze.

HOW IT WORKS

The water pressure pushes all the excess air from the plastic bag, leaving it vacuum packed.

CLEAR THE AIR

For another simple way to vacuum seal food inside a resealable plastic bag, gently squeeze the bag to remove at much air as possible and then seal the bag shut, leaving a small opening. Insert a drinking straw into the hole. Suck out the excess air through the straw, remove the straw, and seal the bag securely. Never use this method if the bag contains uncooked meat, fish, or poultry.

2

COOKWARE AND TABLEWARE

I'm standing at the stove, simmering tomato sauce in pan, stirring every so often with a wooden spoon. The phone rings.

I don't own a ceramic spoon rest, and I'm too lazy to grab a saucer from the cupboard, so I set the wooden spoon in the tomato sauce and rest the handle on the rim of the saucepan. The moment I step away to answer the phone, the wooden spoon slides into the tomato sauce.

Wrong number. In more ways than one.

I fish out the wooden spoon and rinse off the tomato sauce. Still too lazy to grab a saucer from the cupboard, I reach for my Swiss Army knife and carve a notch in the handle of the wooden spoon. Now, whenever I lay the wooden spoon on the rim of a pot or saucepan, the notch secures it in place.

For some people, *necessity* is the mother of invention. For me, it's *laziness*.

How to Make an Apron from a Trash Bag

WHAT YOU NEED

- Tall plastic 13-gallon kitchen trash bag
- Ruler
- Indelible marker
- Scissors

WHAT TO DO

1. Lay the plastic kitchen trash bag on the countertop with the sealed end facing away from you and the open end facing toward you.
2. Fold the trash bag in half lengthwise, with the folded side facing left.
3. Using the ruler and starting from the right-hand edge of the bag, measure 6 inches across the top edge of the bag. Use the indelible marker to mark the spot with a dot.
4. Starting from the top edge of the bag, measure 6 inches down the right-hand edge, and mark the spot with a dot.
5. Using the ruler for guidance, draw a diagonal line to connect the two dots.
6. Starting from the right-hand edge of the bag, measure 7 inches across the top edge of the bag, and mark the spot with a dot.
7. Starting from the top edge of the bag, measure 7 inches down the right-hand edge, and mark the spot with a dot.
8. Using the ruler for guidance, draw a diagonal line to connect the two dots.
9. Starting from the right-hand edge of the bag, measure 1 inch across the bottom edge, and mark the spot with a dot.
10. Starting from the bottom edge of the bag, measure 12 inches up the right-hand edge, and mark the spot with a dot.
11. Starting from the dot you just made on the right-hand side of the bag, measure 1 inch to the left and mark the spot with a dot.
12. Using the ruler and indelible marker, draw a vertical line to connect the dot you just made with the dot along the bottom edge of the bag.

13. With the scissors, carefully cut through all four layers of plastic, to cut off the triangle in the top right-hand corner formed by the shorter diagonal line.

14. Starting on the right-hand edge of the bag, use the scissors to cut through all four layers of plastic along the second diagonal line, stopping 1 inch from the top edge of the bag to form the neck ties for the apron.

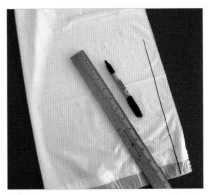

15. From the bottom edge of the bag, use the scissors to cut through all four layers of plastic along the 12-inch vertical line 1 inch from the right to form the waist ties.

16. Unfold the bag.

17. Holding the 2-ply apron to your chest, tie the ends of the neck straps behind your neck.

18. With the plastic apron covering your chest and abdomen, tie the waist ties behind your back.

HOW IT WORKS

Heavy-duty plastic trash bags are tough, durable, and waterproof—protecting your clothes from splashes and spills. **Do not wear the plastic apron near a hot stove or oven.** The plastic will melt or catch fire and may cause burns or other injuries.

BAG OF TRICKS

- You can also improvise an apron by wrapping a belt around your waist to hold a dish towel in place.

How to Season Cast-Iron Cookware with Vegetable Shortening

WHAT YOU NEED
- Paper towel
- Vegetable shortening
- Oven, preheated to 200° Fahrenheit

WHAT TO DO
1. Use a sheet of paper towel to rub vegetable shortening into the interior surface of the cast-iron cookware to create a thin coating.
2. Bake the cookware in an oven heated to 200° Fahrenheit for 2 hours.
3. Remove the cookware from the oven, and let cool to room temperature.
4. Wipe the cookware clean with a fresh sheet of paper towel.
5. After using the new cookware a few times, repeat this procedure.
6. To reseason the cast-iron cookware after each use, use a sheet of paper towel to run a dab of vegetable shortening on the inside of the pot or pan. Wipe off the excess.

HOW IT WORKS
Cast iron needs to be seasoned because the metal is porous. The vegetable shortening seals the pores.

OPEN SEASON
- Seasoning cast-iron cookware prevents rust and creates a natural, permanent nonstick cooking surface.

- To prevent cast-iron pots and pans from rusting, place a sheet of paper towel, a coffee filter, or a sheet of waxed paper inside each cast-iron pot and pan in the cupboard. The paper towel or coffee filter absorbs excess moisture that would otherwise rust the skillets. Replace the paper towel and coffee filter after each use.
- You can also reseason cast-iron cookware with vegetable oil or cooking spray, then wipe clean with a sheet of paper towel.
- Using your cast-iron cookware frequently allows the pan to develop a shiny black patina, making the surface nonstick.

EVERY TRICK IN THE BOOK
Greasing the Wheels

You can also use vegetable shortening to:

- **Break in a New Cake Pan.** Grease the tin with vegetable shortening and warm in an oven set on moderate heat for 15 minutes. Conditioning the pan this way will prevent the bottom of the cake from burning.
- **Preserve a Wooden Cutting Board.** See page 28.
- **Preserve a Wooden Rolling Pin.** Rub a few dabs of vegetable shortening into the wood, let sit overnight, and wipe off the excess shortening with a sheet of paper towel.
- **Season a Wok Before Cooking.** Use a sheet of paper towel to run a dab of vegetable shortening on the inside of the wok. Wipe off the excess.
- **Revitalize and Seal a Wooden Salad Bowl.** Rub vegetable shortening all over the inside and outside of the bowl. Let sit overnight to give the wood time to absorb the shortening, and then use paper towels to remove the excess shortening and buff.
- **Prevent Tomato Sauce and Other Foods from Staining New Wooden Cooking Spoons.** Rub a dollop of vegetable shortening into the wood, let sit overnight, and buff well with a sheet of paper towel. The shortening seals the wood.

How to Preserve a Wooden Cutting Board with Cooking Oil

WHAT YOU NEED

- Paper towel
- Vegetable oil (or vegetable shortening)

WHAT TO DO

1. To preserve a wooden cutting board, saturate a paper towel with vegetable oil (or vegetable shortening).
2. Rub the oil (or shortening) into all sides of the board until the wood cannot absorb any more.
3. Let sit overnight to allow the wood to absorb the oil (or shortening).
4. In the morning, use paper towels to wipe off the excess oil (or shortening).
5. Repeat every three months.

HOW IT WORKS

The vegetable oil (or shortening) nourishes and seals the porous wood, preventing it from drying out and cracking.

EVERY TRICK IN THE BOOK

Burning the Midnight Oil

You can also use vegetable oil to:

- **Separate Drinking Glasses Stuck Inside Each Other.** Dribble a few drops of vegetable oil between the glasses, wait a few seconds, and gently pull them apart.
- **Preserve a Wooden Salad Bowl and Wooden Cooking Spoons.** Follow the same directions as for preserving a cutting board.
- **Clean Caked-On Food from the Blades of a Blender.** Soak the blades in vegetable oil overnight, and in the morning, carefully wash them clean with hot soapy water.

How to Deodorize a Garbage Pail with Kitty Litter

WHAT YOU NEED
- Kitty litter
- Plastic trash bag

WHAT TO DO
1. To absorb moisture from the bottom of a kitchen garbage pail and prevent odors, pour a 1-inch layer of kitty litter on the bottom of the empty trash pail.
2. Line the inside of the trash pail with a plastic trash bag.

HOW IT WORKS
The absorbent clay in the kitty litter absorbs moisture. Some cat-box fillers contain a microencapsulated deodorant system or chemicals that fight odor-causing bacteria.

TRASHY IDEAS
- **Baking Soda.** To deodorize smelly garbage in the kitchen garbage pail, sprinkle a handful of baking soda into the pail every time you add food scraps.

- **Borax.** To inhibit mold and bacteria from growing in a garbage pail, sprinkle ½ cup of borax onto the bottom of the pail.
- **Fabric Softener Sheet.** To neutralize odors in a kitchen garbage pail, place a sheet of fabric softener in the bottom of the pail before lining with a plastic trash bag.
- **Paper Towels.** Place a sheet of paper towel on the bottom of the kitchen garbage pail to absorb moisture and prevent mold and mildew odors.

How to Sharpen a Knife with Sandpaper

WHAT YOU NEED

- Scissors
- One sheet of sandpaper (for best results, use 1,000-grit silicon carbide sandpaper)
- White school glue
- Block of wood (roughly 2 inches x 4 inches x 6 inches)

- Dishwashing liquid
- Water

WHAT TO DO

1. Using scissors, carefully cut a sheet of sandpaper to 4 inches x 6 inches.
2. Use white school glue to attach the trimmed sheet of sandpaper to the block of wood.
3. Let dry overnight.
4. Hold the dull knife at a 90-degree angle to the wooden block, then tilt it halfway down to 45 degrees, then halfway down again to roughly 22.5 degrees.

5. Carefully slide the blade of the knife away from you, keeping the sharp edge flush with the sandpaper. After each slide, lift the blade from the sandpaper and return the blade to its starting position.
6. Slide the knife a dozen times.
7. Flip the knife over and repeat with the opposite side a dozen times.
8. Wash the knife with soapy water before using.

HOW IT WORKS

Sandpaper removes metal from the knife, sharpening the blade.

LOOK SHARP

- In a pinch, you can sharpen a kitchen knife with a porcelain plate. Simply place the plate upside down on the countertop, hold the blade at a 22.5-degree

angle against the raised, unglazed ceramic ring (with the blade facing away from you), and slide the knife toward you ten times. Repeat with the opposite side of the blade. Wash the knife before using.

- To sharpen a pair of kitchen scissors, fold a sheet of aluminum foil in half. Fold the sheet in half again, creating four layers of aluminum foil. Cut through the four layers of aluminum foil with the scissors a dozen or more times.

- To clean any sticky residue from the blades of a knife or kitchen scissors, soak a cotton ball with vodka and carefully wipe the blades clean.

WHEN DO WE EAT?
How to Improvise a Measuring Cup

- **Coffee Mug.** The standard coffee mug holds 12 fluid ounces.
- **Coffeemaker Carafe.** Twelve 1-cup markings are generally printed in white ink on the side of the glass coffee pot.
- **Ice Cube Tray.** Each compartment in an ice cube tray holds 1 fluid ounce.
- **Paper Cup.** An all-purpose Dixie cup holds 5 ounces of liquid.
- **Red Solo Cup.** On the iconic red drinking cup of fraternity parties, the bottom line corresponds to 1 ounce, the middle line equals 5 ounces, and the third line from the top is 12 ounces.
- **Shot Glass.** A standard American shot glass holds 1½ fluid ounces.
- **Soup Can.** An empty Campbell's Soup can holds 11 fluid ounces.
- **Whiskey Glass.** The typical 10½-ounce American whiskey glass, when filled three-quarters full, measures roughly 1 cup.
- **Yogurt Cup.** A clean, empty yogurt cup holds 6 fluid ounces.

How to Improvise a Meat Mallet with a Frying Pan

WHAT YOU NEED
- Waxed paper
- Cutting board
- Frying pan, cast-iron or simply heavy

WHAT TO DO

1. Place the meat or boned chicken breast between two sheets of waxed paper on top of a cutting board.
2. Hammer the covered meat or chicken breast with the bottom of a cast-iron or heavy frying pan to flatten it.

HOW IT WORKS

The weight of the frying pan and its flat bottom helps the skillet double as a hammer. The waxed paper prevents the meat juices from splattering.

START WITH A BANG

- Rather than beating a piece of tough meat with a meat mallet, roll a pizza cutter over each side of the meat.
- Other great substitutes for a meat mallet include a rolling pin, an empty wine bottle, a can of tomatoes, a baseball bat, a cutting board, or a really heavy hardcover novel (ideally wrapped in plastic wrap).

WHEN DO WE EAT?
How to Open a Stubborn Jar

- **Blow-Dryer.** Turn the blow-dryer on warm and heat the lid. Heat expands and so will the lid, loosening it from the jar. If the lid is glued to the rim of the jar by some sticky food, the heat from the blow-dryer will melt the culprit.

- **Petroleum Jelly.** After opening a jar of a sticky food like honey, jam, maple syrup, or molasses, rub a thin coat of petroleum jelly around the rim of the jar to make the lid easier to remove next time.
- **Rubber Gloves.** Put on a pair of rubber kitchen gloves to give your hands the traction they need to twist off the top.
- **Sandpaper.** Cover the lid of the jar or bottle top with a sheet of sandpaper and twist. The abrasive sandpaper creates enough friction to give you a good grasp.

How to Stack China and Nonstick Cookware with Paper Plates

WHAT YOU NEED
- Paper plates

WHAT TO DO
1. To prevent china or nonstick cookware from getting scratched, place a paper plate on the inside bottoms of all the cookware.
2. Stack the prepared pots and pans on top of each other.

HOW IT WORKS
The paper plates prevent the fragile surfaces of the china or nonstick cookware from touching each other directly, preventing scratches.

HOW TO STACK CHINA
- To put paper plates between china bowls, use a pair of scissor to carefully cut some lines a few inches deep into the paper plate, like spokes of a bicycle wheel. The lines allow the paper plate to collapse into the shape of the bowl.
- Before washing fine china and crystal in the sink, place a dishtowel on the bottom of the sink to create a cushion to avoid nicks and chips.
- If you don't have paper plates, place a sheet of paper towel or a round coffee filter between each china plate to protect them in the cupboard.

How to Protect Plastic Containers from Tomato Stains with Cooking Spray

WHAT YOU NEED
- Cooking spray

WHAT TO DO
1. Before filling the plastic container with any food containing tomatoes, spray the inside of the container with cooking spray.

HOW IT WORKS
The lecithin in the cooking spray repels the pigments that would otherwise stain the plastic.

STAIN PAIN
- Another way to prevent stains inside a plastic container (and stop foul odors from permeating the plastic): line the container with a sheet of plastic wrap before adding the food item.
- If the inside of a plastic container gets stained with tomato sauce, fill the container with warm water and add 1 tablespoon of bleach for

every cup of water. Let sit for 30 minutes, rinse clean, and dry. Or fill the containers with hot water, drop in two denture cleansing tablets, and let sit overnight. In the morning, wash with soapy water, rinse clean, and dry.

- For another way to bleach tomato sauce stains from plastic containers, apply lemon juice to the stain and place the open container in the sun for a few hours. Rinse clean and dry.

EVERY TRICK IN THE BOOK
A Quick Spritz

You can also use cooking spray to:

- **Pry Apart Two Drinking Glasses Stuck Inside Each Other.** Spray some cooking spray between the two glasses, allow the oil to seep in, and softly tug the glasses apart.
- **Prevent Paper Liners from Sticking to Cupcakes.** Before filling paper liners with cupcake batter, spray the inside of the liners with cooking spray.
- **Make Sticky Ingredients Glide Out of Measuring Spoons and Cups.** Spray the bowls of measuring spoons and the insides of measuring cups with cooking spray so honey, molasses, chocolate syrup, or corn syrup slide right out, making cleanup effortless.
- **Prevent Cookie Dough from Sticking to Your Hands.** Before shaping cookie dough into cookies, give your hands a light coat of cooking spray.
- **Stop Berry Juice from Staining Your Hands.** Before working with berries, give your hands with a light coat of cooking spray.
- **Season Popcorn with Salt or Garlic Powder.** Before adding the seasoning, give the popcorn a light coat of cooking spray. The salt or garlic powder will stick to the oil.

How to Protect Oven Mitts and Pot Holders with Spray Starch

WHAT YOU NEED
- Waxed paper
- Aerosol spray starch

WHAT TO DO

1. To prevent oven mitts and pot holders from getting soiled with grease and oil stains from cooking, place the oven mitt or pot holder on a sheet of waxed paper.

2. Spray the item with a protective coat of spray starch. Let it sit for 1 minute.
3. Flip over the item and spray the remaining side. Let it sit for another minute.
4. Discard the waxed paper.

HOW IT WORKS

The starch prevents the fabric of the oven mitt or pot holder from absorbing stains.

A HELPING HAND
- Improvise an oven mitt with work gloves, welding mitts, ski gloves, two socks, or even a thick Christmas stocking.
- Create an impromptu pot holder by folding a dish towel in quarters.
- An oven mitt doubles as a beverage cozy. To keep a cup of coffee or tea warm, place an oven mitt over the cup.
- Hard-boiled eggs will stay warm for up to 30 minutes if placed inside an oven mitt.

How to Improvise a Funnel

The following items can be turned into an impromptu funnel:

- **Aluminum Foil.** Cut a square sheet of aluminum foil, fold it in half, and then fold it in half a second time. Using a pair of scissors, snip off the folded corner, and open one of the flaps to create a funnel.
- **Bleach Jug.** Cut a clean, empty bleach jug in half horizontally, turn the upper half upside down, and remove the cap.
- **Paper Cup.** Punch a hole in the bottom of a paper cup near the outer edge.
- **Resealable Plastic Bag.** Using a pair of scissor, snip off one of the bottom corners from a resealable plastic bag.
- **Soda Bottle.** Cut the bottom half off a clean, empty 1-liter plastic soda bottle, turn the upper half upside down, and remove the cap.

How to Improvise a Rolling Pin with a Wine Bottle and Panty Hose

WHAT YOU NEED

- A full, cold wine bottle
- Dishwashing liquid
- Water
- Towel
- Scissors
- A clean, used pair of panty hose
- Waxed paper (optional)

WHAT TO DO

1. Wash the outside of the wine bottle well with dishwashing liquid and water.
2. Dry the wine bottle with a towel.
3. Using the scissors, carefully cut off one leg of the pair of panty hose at the knee.
4. Insert the full, cold bottle into the panty hose leg until it reaches the toe.

5. Tie a knot in the panty hose at the end of the bottle.
6. Use the scissors to trim the excess panty hose at the knot.
7. Roll the wrapped bottle over kneaded dough like a rolling pin.
8. If you are unable to wash the bottle or don't have panty hose available, place the dough between two sheets of waxed paper and roll the wine bottle over it.
9. Rub a handful of flour on the nylon to prevent the dough from sticking to it.

HOW IT WORKS

The abrasive nylon of the panty hose helps the bottle glide over the dough without sticking to the glass bottle.

READY TO ROLL

- To prevent foods from sticking to a rolling pin, spray the roller with a fine coat of cooking spray.
- To neutralize strong odors and remove stains from a wooden rolling pin, rub lemon juice over the pin and then roll it through a mountain of salt. Wash the pin in warm, soapy water, rinse clean, and dry. The lemon juice bleaches the stains and deodorizes, and the abrasive salt absorbs odors and grease.

EVERY TRICK IN THE BOOK
You're on a Roll

Other great substitutes for a rolling pin:

- **Baseball Bat.** Wash an aluminum baseball bat thoroughly with soap and water, and—*viola!*—you've got a rolling pin that doubles as a meat mallet.
- **Broomstick.** Most modern-day broomsticks unscrew from the bristles, and in a pinch, the broomstick can be used as rolling pin.
- **PVC Pipe.** A 12-inch length of PVC pipe (ideally with a diameter greater than 1 inch) doubles as a rolling pin.
- **Soda Can.** A full soda can works well as a rolling pin. An empty can will crush.
- **Thermos Bottle.** A tall thermos bottle is just the right diameter to do the work of a rolling pin.
- **Water Bottle.** A sturdy water bottle, filled with water, works as a rolling pin.

How to Remove Contact Paper with a Blow-Dryer

WHAT YOU NEED
- Blow-dryer
- Extension cord (if necessary)
- Putty knife
- Rag (or paper towel)
- Isopropyl rubbing alcohol

WHAT TO DO
1. To lift old contact paper from pantry shelves, plug in the blow-dryer near the shelf, using an extension cord if needed.
2. Turn on the blow-dryer to its highest heat setting.
3. Aim the nozzle of the blow-dryer at one corner of the contact paper, holding it roughly 3 inches above the surface for 30 to 60 seconds.
4. Gently lift the corner of the contact paper with a putty knife and slowly peel back a small section of the paper at a 180-degree angle. Pulling back flat against the existing contact paper puts the least stress on the paper, preventing it from tearing.
5. Continually moving the blow-dryer over the nearby surface of the contact paper, warm a 1-foot-square area of the contact paper (roughly the size of an 8½-inch x 11-inch sheet of paper).
6. Carefully peel back as much contact paper as possible.
7. Repeat steps 4 and 5 until you've removed all the contact paper.
8. Use a rag or paper towel dampened with isopropyl rubbing alcohol to clean any remaining patches of adhesive from the shelf.

HOW IT WORKS
The heat from the blow-dryer melts the adhesive backing holding the contact paper in place, allowing you to peel it from the shelf with ease.

STICKY SITUATIONS
- To remove chewing gum from hair, clothes, carpet, or upholstery, rub a dollop of creamy peanut butter into the gum, let sit for 5 minutes, and comb or brush out (using a toothbrush if necessary). The oils in the peanut butter dissolve the adhesives in the chewing gum.

- To remove any adhesive residue from a label or price sticker from plastic containers, mirrors, or picture frames, rub a dab of creamy peanut butter into the adhesive and let sit 5 minutes. The oils in the peanut butter soften and loosen the adhesive. Wipe clean.

EVERY TRICK IN THE BOOK

Full of Hot Air

You can also use a blow-dryer to:

- **Defrost a Freezer.** Using an extension cord if necessary, wave the nozzle of a blow-dryer turned on its highest heat setting at the ice—holding the device roughly 6 inches away to avoid getting the blow-dryer wet.
- **Dry Strawberries Before Dipping in Chocolate.** After rinsing the strawberries gently in a colander, place them on a clean dish towel, lay a second dish towel on top, and pat gently. Remove the top towel, set a blow-dryer on cool, and dry the berries.
- **Set Icing on a Cake.** See page 164.
- **Soften Ice Cream.** If a container of ice cream is too frozen to scoop, set a blow-dryer on warm and gently defrost the container.
- **Make Creamier Mashed Potatoes.** After draining boiled potatoes to be mashed, set a blow-dryer on warm, and blow the wet potatoes until they dry.
- **Remove Candle Wax from a Table, Countertop, or Candleholder.** Aim the nozzle of a blow-dryer set on warm at the dried wax and use a paper towel to wipe up the softened wax.
- **Prevent Water Spots on a Recently Cleaned Crystal Vase.** Using a blow-dryer, blow warm air inside the mouth of the vase until the remaining water droplets dry.
- **Unclog a Sink.** The clog tends to be located in the bottom of the trap under the sink. Aim the nozzle of a blow dryer set on high at the trap, allowing the heat to warm the pipe and melt the coagulated grease. Then run hot water to flush the melted grease through the pipe.

How to Improvise a Food Strainer with Panty Hose

WHAT YOU NEED

- Scissors
- Clean, used pair of panty hose
- Pot or bowl

WHAT TO DO

1. Using the scissors, carefully cut off one leg of the pair of panty hose at the top of the thigh.
2. Stretch the opening across the mouth of a pot or bowl.
3. Pour the food into the open leg.
4. Lift up the panty hose leg over the pot or bowl and squeeze the food through the nylon mesh into the vessel.

HOW IT WORKS

The fine nylon netting acts like a strainer.

DON'T STRAIN YOURSELF

- A reusable gold mesh coffee filter doubles as a strainer.
- If you don't have a colander, use an ice pick to punch holes in the bottom of an aluminum pie plate.
- In a pinch, a sheet of cheesecloth (or several layers of cheesecloth) can be used as a strainer.
- If your tea bag breaks in a cup of tea, lace two layers of paper towel over a second cup, and pour the tea through the paper towels, allowing the paper to catch the tea leaves.

- Insert a tennis racket into a pair of clean panty hose to strain a pot of cooked spaghetti noodles. The nylon mesh prevents the noodles from slipping through the webbing.
- In a real emergency, a clean window screen can be used as a sieve.

Strain Away

You can also use a food strainer to:

- **Steam Vegetables.** Set a strainer in a pot filled with an inch of simmering water, place chopped vegetables in the strainer, and cover with a lid. Make sure the water doesn't boil from the pot before the vegetables finish steaming.
- **Squeeze Juice from Citrus Fruits.** Place a strainer over a bowl or drinking glass, and squeeze the lemon, lime, or orange. The mesh catches the seeds and pulp, leaving only juice in the bowl or glass.
- **Sift Dry Ingredients.** Place the strainer over your mixing bowl, pour your measured ingredients into the strainer, and gently tap the strainer to get rid of any lumps or clumps.
- **Prevent Spatters from Frying Bacon.** Place a fine mesh strainer upside down over the pan of frying bacon to catch sputtering hot grease.
- **Strain Homemade Cheese.** Extract the curds from homemade cheese by using a large metal spoon to press the cheese through a fine-mesh strainer. For ricotta cheese, place a double layer of paper towels in the strainer before proceeding.
- **Powder Cookies, Cakes, Brownies, or Pies.** Place confectioners' sugar or cocoa into a strainer and, holding it a foot above the dessert, tap the side to dust the desert.

How to Protect a Teapot Spout with a Rubber Glove

WHAT YOU NEED
- Scissors
- Clean, used rubber kitchen glove

WHAT TO DO
1. Using a pair of scissors, carefully cut off a finger from a rubber kitchen glove.
2. Place the rubber fingertip over the spout of the teapot.

HOW IT WORKS
The rubber finger from the glove provides protective padding, safeguarding the teapot spout from unsightly chips.

HANDS DOWN
- Wearing rubber gloves while washing the dishes can irritate skin. Sprinkle baby powder or cornstarch inside the gloves to reduce friction against the skin and to help the gloves slip on and off easily.

- To extend the life of rubber kitchen gloves, stuff a cotton ball into each fingertip of the gloves to prevent your fingernails from tearing through the tips.
- Improvise rubber gloves by placing each hand inside its own resealable plastic bag.

EVERY TRICK IN THE BOOK

Fingers Crossed

You can also use rubber gloves to:

- **Make an Ice Pack.** Fill a rubber kitchen glove with ice, tie the cuff securely to prevent leaks, and apply to around the affected area for 10 minutes to relieve pain.
- **Moisturize Your Hands.** Apply skin cream to your hands, then put on a pair of rubber kitchen gloves and do the dishes. The heat from the warm water will help the cream penetrate your skin.
- **Protect Your Skin from Hot Peppers.** When cutting up jalapeño peppers, put a rubber kitchen glove on each hand to keep the caustic heat from the peppers—which doesn't wash off easily—from getting on your skin.
- **Shield Yourself from Skunk Spray.** If you're washing the smell of skunk from a child or a family pet, be sure to wear rubber kitchen gloves to avoid getting the skunk smell all over yourself.
- **Make Jumbo Rubber Bands.** When your rubber kitchen gloves wear out, use a pair of scissors to slice up the cuff to make large rubber bands.
- **Make a Finger Grip for Sorting Through Papers.** Cut off a fingertip from a clean, old rubber kitchen glove and slip it over your index or middle finger to sort through papers.

- **Prevent the End of a Broom or Mop Handle from Scratching or Marking Walls.** Cut off a finger from a clean, used pair of rubber kitchen gloves and slip the finger over the end of the broom or mop handle.
- **Remove Pet Hair from Furniture.** Put on a pair of rubber gloves, fill a bucket halfway with water, dip the gloves in the water, wipe the area affected by the pet hair, and dip the gloves in the water again. The wet rubber attracts the pet hair, and the water rinses it off.
- **Prevent Pliers from Leaving Marks.** Cut off two fingers from a clean, used pair of rubber gloves and slip them over the jaws of pliers as protective padding.

3

APPLIANCES AND GADGETS

Running late one morning, I stepped into the kitchen determined to cook a hard-boiled egg as quickly as possible. I grabbed an egg from the refrigerator, placed it on a saucer, put it in the microwave oven, and set the timer for 1 minute.

Little did I realize, the microwaves concentrated the heat in the center of the egg, prompting the yolk to release steam, creating massive pressure inside the shell.

Within 30 seconds, the egg exploded, coating the inside of the microwave oven with broken eggshells and gooey raw egg.

That night I did something I'd never done before. I sat down and read the instruction manual.

How to Ignite a Charcoal Barbecue with a Coffee Can

WHAT YOU NEED

- Can opener
- Clean, empty coffee can
- Tin snips
- One sheet of newspaper
- Charcoal briquettes
- Butane barbecue lighter (or barbecue matches)
- Metal tongs

WHAT TO DO

1. With the can opener, carefully remove the top and bottom of the clean, empty coffee can.
2. Using the tin snips, carefully cut several 1-inch-tall triangular slots equidistant around the bottom rim of the coffee can as shown above.
3. Remove the cooking grate from your barbecue grill.
4. Stand the can with the slots downward in the center of the charcoal grate in your barbecue grill.

5. Crumble up a sheet of newspaper and place it inside the can.
6. Fill the rest of the can with charcoal briquettes.
7. Using the butane barbecue lighter (or barbecue matches), light the newspaper through one of the triangular slots.
8. When the coals glow orange and the top ones turn gray with ash (typically after 10 to 15 minutes), use a pair of tongs to carefully remove the hot can, and set it in a safe place until it cools.

9. Using the tongs, carefully arrange the coals to your liking on the charcoal grate.
10. Set the cooking grate back in place and close the lid.
11. Wait 10 to 15 minutes for the grill to heat up sufficiently (reaching 500° to 550° Fahrenheit).
12. Cook.

HOW IT WORKS

You've created a homemade charcoal chimney. The coffee can holds the charcoal briquettes tightly together for better combustion. The triangular slots around the bottom rim of the coffee can allow oxygen to flow abundantly, making the coals burn hot and fast.

WHAT'S COOKING

- Prevent grease fires in a charcoal barbecue grill by covering the bottom of the pan with an even layer of unused kitty litter to absorb grease and fat drippings.
- To ignite a fire in a charcoal barbecue, apply a thick coat of petroleum jelly to a cotton ball, place it amid the charcoal, and light.
- To fan the flames of a recently ignited charcoal fire in a barbecue grill, point the nozzle of a blow-dryer set on cool at the flames until the charcoal briquettes catch fire.
- Before placing pots or pans on a barbecue grill, coat the bottom of the cookware with shaving cream. When you finish grilling, the black soot will wash off the bottom of the pots and pans with ease.
- After barbecuing in a charcoal grill, sprinkle salt over the smoldering charcoal to prevent a grease fire from suddenly bursting into flames.

EVERY TRICK IN THE BOOK
Can Do

You can also use a coffee can to:

- **Store Dry Food.** Keep beans, flour, and sugar in a clean, empty coffee can, appropriately labeled, with the plastic lid tightly sealed.
- **Wrap Cookies and Candies.** Cover an empty coffee can with wrapping paper, fill with cookies or candy, cover with the plastic lid, then wrap.
- **Improvise a Gelatin Mold.** Fill a clean, empty coffee can with gelatin.

How to Clean a Coffee Grinder or Food Processor with Rice

WHAT YOU NEED

- 1 cup of rice
- Boiling water
- Dishwashing liquid
- Ice cubes

WHAT TO DO

Coffee Grinder:

1. Run 1 cup of rice through the grinder.

Food Processor:

1. Fill the bowl of the food processor with rice and pulverize it.
2. Discard the rice.
3. Carefully fill the food processor bowl halfway with boiling water.
4. Add a few drops of dishwashing liquid.
5. Let the solution sit until the water cools.
6. Add a handful of ice cubes, secure the lid in place, and process for 30 seconds.
7. Rinse clean and dry thoroughly.

HOW IT WORKS

The rice flushes coffee bean residue from the grinder, deodorizes the bowl of the food processor, sharpens the blades, and absorbs foul odors.

KEEP IT CLEAN

- Another way to eliminate food odors from a coffee grinder or food processor bowl: run several slices of white bread through the device.
- To clean tight crevices on the outside of a food processor or between the push buttons, dip a toothpick in rubbing alcohol, work it along the tight spaces, and then scrub with a clean, old toothbrush.
- To avoid having to clean the food processor lid, place the food in the bowl, cover the bowl with a sheet of plastic wrap, and secure the lid in place. After processing the food, remove the clean lid and discard the spattered plastic wrap.

How to Clean a Coffeemaker or Teakettle with Vinegar

WHAT YOU NEED

- 1 gallon of white vinegar
- Water
- Dishwashing liquid

WHAT TO DO

1. To clean mineral deposits encrusted on the heating elements of a coffeemaker or a teakettle, fill the water reservoir with white vinegar.
2. Run the vinegar through the regular brewing cycle—with the coffeepot in place.
3. Repeat if necessary.
4. Run fresh water through the machine twice to rinse out any vinegar residue.
5. Wash the coffeepot with a few drops of dishwashing liquid and water.

HOW IT WORKS

The acetic acid in the vinegar dissolves the mineral deposits.

CLEAN AS A WHISTLE

- Clean coffee residue from inside a glass coffeepot by pouring equal parts baking soda and lemon juice into the pot and scrubbing with a sponge. Or pour ½ cup of salt into the empty coffeepot, fill with ice cubes, and swirl the coffeepot so that the ice cubes whirl around inside it, scrubbing the stains with the abrasive salt.
- To clean the coffee filter basket, remove the basket, fill the kitchen sink with soapy water, add ¼ cup of white vinegar, and soak the basket in the solution for 30 minutes. Rinse clean.

- Clean tea stains from the inside of a teapot by filling the teapot with warm water and dropping in two denture cleansing tablets. Let sit for 2 hours and rinse clean.

WHEN DO WE EAT?

Cooking with a Coffeemaker

- **Hard-Boiled Eggs.** Gently place however many eggs you'd like in the coffeepot. A 12-cup coffeemaker will hold four to six eggs. Fill the coffeemaker reservoir with fresh water, close the lid, and turn on the coffeemaker. Let the hot water run through the machine and fill the coffeepot. Once the eggs are submerged in hot water, let the eggs sit in the coffeepot on the burner for 10 to 12 minutes for hard-boiled eggs (5 to 6 minutes for soft-boiled eggs). Carefully pour the hot water down the sink, and pour cold water over the hard-boiled eggs to let them cool.

- **Hot Dogs.** Fill the reservoir in the coffeemaker with 6 to 8 cups of water, place a few defrosted hot dogs in the coffeepot, turn on the coffeemaker, and after the water fills the coffeepot, let the hotdogs heat in the water for 30 to 45 minutes.

- **Ramen.** Using the coffeepot, place 2 cups of water in the reservoir of the coffeemaker. Crush the ramen noodles inside the packet to make smaller pieces that cook quicker. Place the noodles in the coffeepot and add the seasoning from the packet. Run the water through the coffeemaker, and carefully pour the finished soup into a bowl.

- **Rice.** To make two servings, pour 1 cup of water in the coffeemaker reservoir. Place 1 cup of instant rice in the coffeepot, and place the coffeepot on the burner. Run the water through the coffeemaker, and let the coffeepot sit on the burner for 5 to 10 minutes or until the rice is fluffy.

- **Steamed Vegetables.** Place the washed, cut vegetables (broccoli, carrots, green beans, etc.) in the coffee filter basket, fill the coffeepot with water, and run the water through the coffeemaker several times until the vegetables are tender. Or place the vegetables in the coffeepot, fill with hot water, and heat on the burner until tender.

For more recipes, visit www.cookingwithyourcoffeemaker.com.

How to Clean a Dishwasher with Kool-Aid

WHAT YOU NEED
- 1 packet of Kool-Aid drink mix (ideally lemon, lime, or orange)

WHAT TO DO
1. Empty all the dishes and utensils from the dishwasher.
2. Empty one packet of Kool-Aid drink mix into the detergent reservoir.
3. Close the door, and run the dishwasher through its regular cycle.

HOW IT WORKS
The citric acid in the Kool-Aid cleans the soap scum from the pipes and tubes of a dishwasher and the grime and rust stains from the inside walls of the machine. The citrus-flavored drink mix also eliminates nasty smells.

EVERY TRICK IN THE BOOK
Washed Up

You can also use these secret tips to clean dishes:

- **Remove Caked-On Food from Dishes.** Sprinkle ¼ cup of baking soda on the floor of the dishwasher before running the machine.
- **Eliminate Soapy Film from Dishes and Glassware.** Vinegar removes soap scum. Place a bowl containing 2 cups of white vinegar on the bottom rack of your dishwasher and run the machine for 5 minutes— without any detergent. Then add the detergent, and run the dishes and glasses though the regular cycle.

- **Lubricate Dishwasher Racks.** Spray the rollers with cooking spray, an edible, nontoxic vegetable oil, so they roll back and forth with ease.

WHEN DO WE EAT?

Cooking with a Dishwasher

Chef Bob Blumer, creator and host of the television show *The Surreal Gourmet* on the Food Network and the author of four cookbooks, devised this recipe (based on an urban legend) for a moist and perfectly cooked salmon fillet. Since then, Bob has poached salmon in more than 100 dishwashers on three continents.

DISHWASHER SALMON

What You Need

- Heavy-duty aluminum foil
- 2 tablespoons of olive oil
- 4 salmon fillets, 6 ounces each
- 4 tablespoons of freshly squeezed lime juice
- Salt and freshly ground black pepper to taste
- 2 sprigs of fresh dill

What to Do

1. Cut two 12-inch pieces of heavy-duty aluminum foil.
2. Grease the shiny side of the foil with the oil. Place two salmon fillets side by side on each square and fold up the outer edges.
3. Pour 1 tablespoon of lime juice over each fillet. Season with salt and pepper, and top with dill.
4. Fold and pinch the aluminum foil extra tightly to create a water-tight seal around each pair of fillets.
5. Place the foil packets on the top rack of the empty dishwasher for the entire normal wash and dry cycle.
6. When the cycle is complete, take out the salmon, discard the foil, and place each fillet on a plate.

Le Secret: Make sure the packet is airtight by pressing down on it gently with your hand. If air escapes easily, repackage. And make sure that your dishwasher is on the regular cycle (economy settings will undercook the fish).

Reprinted from Off the Eaten Path: Inspired Recipes for Adventurous Cooks *by Bob Blumer (Ballantine Books). Copyright 2000 by Bob Blumer. Reprinted with permission. All rights reserved. Watch Bob's tutorial at https://www.youtube.com/watch?v=etK3-JTNjdc*

WHEN DO WE EAT?

Things You Can Clean with a Dishwasher

All of these items can be safely washed in a dishwasher through a normal wash cycle (withstanding temperatures up to 170° Fahrenheit) with regular dishwasher detergent —unless otherwise noted below:

- **Baseball Caps.** Place the baseball caps on the top rack.
- **Golf Balls.** Put the golf balls in a mesh sack (or the foot cut from a pair of panty hose), place them on the bottom rack.
- **Hairbrushes and Combs.** Run a comb through the brushes to remove any hair, and place the hairbrushes and combs in the silverware basket.

- **Hubcaps.** Place the hubcaps upright in the bottom rack, add your regular dishwasher detergent to the receptacle dish, and add 1 cup of white vinegar.
- **Kitchen Magnets.** Cut off one foot from a clean, used pair of panty hose, place the kitchen magnets in the foot, knot the open end, and run the magnet-filled sachet through the dishwasher (in the silverware bin or tied to one of the racks).
- **Sponges.** Place sponges in the silverware basket or on the top rack to sanitize them.

- **Tools.** Place wrenches, pliers, and screwdrivers (and any other tools that do not have wooden handles) in the silverware basket. Afterward, immediately dry the tools.
- **Toys.** Place small toys, like Lego pieces and action figures, in a mesh lingerie bag (to avoid losing pieces in the dishwasher) and run through the regular cycle. The dishwasher, reaching temperatures up to 170° Fahrenheit, will sanitize the toys (making them clean and hygienic) but not sterilize them (killing any bacteria and microorganisms).
- **Trivets.** Place trivets upright in the bottom rack to remove grease and grime.

How to Improvise a Salad Spinner with a Pillowcase

WHAT YOU NEED

- Greens
- Colander
- Clean pillowcase
- Large salad bowl

WHAT TO DO

1. Rinse the greens with cool water in a colander.
2. Place the rinsed greens inside the clean pillowcase.
3. Standing outside, grab the end of the pillowcase, and twirl it over your head like a lasso for 60 seconds.
4. Return inside and empty the greens from the damp pillowcase into a large salad bowl.

HOW IT WORKS

The centrifugal force flings the water from the lettuce into the sides of the cotton pillowcase, dampening the cloth.

GOING FOR A SPIN

- Don't have a pillowcase? Use a clean, used pair of panty hose.
- You can also improvise a salad spinner by wrapping the rinsed greens inside several sheets of paper towel. Place the bundle inside a clean, used plastic grocery bag, and standing outside, whirl the bag over your head for 1 minute. The paper towels absorb the flung water.

- You can also dry wet salad greens with a blow-dryer. Simply set the blow-dryer on cool, and blow the wet leaves of the greens, then refrigerate to keep them crisp.

How to Deodorize a Refrigerator or Freezer with Kitty Litter

WHAT YOU NEED

- Measuring spoons
- 1 teaspoon of dishwashing liquid
- Warm water
- Bucket
- Sponge
- Measuring cups
- ¾ cup of bleach
- 1 gallon of water
- Towel
- Kitty litter

- 2 plastic storage containers (approximately 10 inches x 15 inches x 6 inches) or 2 shallow cardboard boxes

WHAT TO DO

1. Unplug the refrigerator and freezer.
2. Mix 1 teaspoon of dishwashing liquid in a gallon of warm water in a bucket.
3. Using a sponge, clean the inside of the appliance with the soapy water.
4. Rinse all inside surfaces with a solution made from ¾ cup bleach and 1 gallon of water.

5. Dry all surfaces with a towel.
6. Pour unused kitty litter in two plastic storage containers (or two shallow cardboard boxes), roughly 2 inches deep.
7. Place one box on the middle shelf in the refrigerator.
8. Place the second box in the freezer.
9. Shut the doors.
10. Plug in the appliance, and keep the doors closed for several days.

HOW IT WORKS

The kitty litter absorbs excess moisture and the foul odor of spoiled food, deodorizing the appliance.

WHAT'S THE BIG STINK?

- Another way to eliminate rancid odors from inside a clean, empty, unplugged refrigerator: after cleaning the inside walls with soapy water, rinsing with bleach, and drying thoroughly with a towel, fill the appliance with crumpled-up pages of newspaper, close the door, and let sit undisturbed for several days. Newsprint absorbs nasty odors.

- Placing a flat, open cardboard box filled with kitty litter in an unplugged refrigerator prevents the unplugged appliance from attracting mold or mildew and the accompanying stench.

- Lining the floor of each crisper drawer with a sheet of paper towel absorbs moisture, keeping fruit and vegetables fresh longer.

WHEN DO WE EAT?

Atypical Things to Store in the Refrigerator

- **Candles.** Keeping taper candles in the refrigerator makes them burn longer. Wrap the candles in plastic wrap or aluminum foil to prevent the wicks from absorbing moisture. While a cold candle burns more slowly than a candle stored at room temperature, the heat from the flame warms a cold candle to room temperature in just a few minutes.

- **Eye Cream.** Placing jars of eye cream in the refrigerator brings down the temperature of the cream, which boosts the cream's ability to eliminate puffy eyes.

- **Eyeliner.** Storing your eyeliner pencil in the refrigerator for 20 minutes before using it allows you to sharpen the pencil to a finer tip and create a more precise line.

- **Flowers.** Keep cut flowers in the refrigerator, just like florists do, to preserve them for an event. If you keep a vase of flowers on display during the day, place them in the refrigerator at night.

How to Deodorize a Garbage Disposal with a Lemon

WHAT YOU NEED
- Sharp kitchen knife
- Lemon
- Cutting board

WHAT TO DO
1. With a sharp kitchen knife, cut a lemon in quarters on a cutting board.
2. Stick the four lemon quarters down into the garbage disposal.
3. With the tap water running, turn on the garbage disposal.
4. Let the disposal run for 30 seconds or until the lemon is completely ground up and washed down the drain.

HOW IT WORKS
The lemon juice deodorizes the garbage disposal.

GARBAGE IN, GARBAGE OUT
- If you prefer not to run lemon rinds through your garbage disposal, put a handful of ice cubes and 2 tablespoons of lemon juice in the disposal and grind for 2 minutes. The ice cubes clean the blades, and the lemon juice deodorizes.
- Another option: fill an ice cube tray with vinegar, freeze (leaving a note on the ice cube tray to prevent mishaps), and grind the ice cubes through the disposal.

EVERY TRICK IN THE BOOK
More Ways to Deodorize a Garbage Disposal
- **Baking Soda.** Pour 1 cup down the drain, flush with water, and repeat with a second cup while running the disposal.
- **Salt.** Pour ½ cup into the garbage disposal, and flush with water for 2 minutes while running the disposal.

How to Deodorize a Microwave Oven with Coffee

WHAT YOU NEED

- Measuring spoons
- 2 tablespoons of ground coffee
- ½ cup of water
- Coffee mug

WHAT TO DO

1. Mix 2 tablespoons of ground coffee and ½ cup of water in a coffee mug.
2. Place the coffee mug in the microwave oven and close the door.
3. Heat on high for 3 minutes.
4. When the microwave oven shuts off, let the coffee mug sit in the oven for 2 minutes.
5. Carefully remove the coffee mug from the microwave oven and discard the coffee.

HOW IT WORKS

Coffee absorbs and masks odors, including the smell of burned popcorn, from a microwave oven.

RAISING A STINK

If the coffee method fails to eliminate the smell of burned popcorn from the microwave oven, try any one of these easy methods:

- **Baking Soda.** Dissolve 2 tablespoons of baking soda in 1 cup of water. Boil the mixture in a bowl or coffee mug in the microwave oven for 5 minutes, allowing the steam to condense on the inside walls of the oven. Wipe clean with a sponge.
- **Lemon Juice.** Mix 2 tablespoons of lemon juice in 1 cup of water, and heat the lemony solution in the microwave oven for 1 minute. With a sponge, wipe the condensation from the walls of the oven.
- **Vanilla Extract.** Pour 1 tablespoon of vanilla extract into a coffee mug, and heat for 30 seconds to 1 minute in the microwave oven. Let the coffee mug sit undisturbed in the microwave with the door sealed shut overnight. In the morning, use a damp sponge to wipe down the inside of the microwave oven.
- **Vinegar.** Unplug the microwave oven, place 1 cup of white vinegar inside the oven, leave the door open, and let sit for at least 24 hours. Vinegar absorbs and neutralizes odors.

WHEN DO WE EAT?
Clever Uses for a Microwave Oven

- **Disinfect a Cutting Board.** After washing the cutting board with soap and water, slice a lemon in half and rub the flesh of the lemon into the cutting board. Place the cutting board in the microwave oven and heat for 1 minute.
- **Disinfect a Used Sponge.** Place the dampened sponge in the microwave oven and heat for 1 minute to disinfect it.
- **Juice Fruits.** If you microwave a citrus fruit for 15 seconds before juicing it, you'll get nearly twice as much juice from the fruit.

- **Liquefy Crystallized Honey.** If honey solidifies inside a jar, use a microwave oven to bring it back to a viscous consistency. Uncover the jar, place it in the microwave oven, and heat for 1 to 3 minutes, stirring every 30 seconds. Honey never spoils, and crystallization does not affect the taste or purity of honey.
- **Peel Garlic Cloves.** Place the garlic cloves on a sheet of paper towel in the microwave oven and heat for 10 seconds. The paper towel absorbs the moisture from the cloves, letting you peel them with ease.
- **Prevent Onions from Causing Tears.** To avoid crying while cutting an onion, heat the onion in the microwave for 30 seconds before chopping it. The heat reduces the sting in the onion juice.
- **Revitalize Stale Potato Chips.** Place a dry dish towel on a dish inside the microwave oven, and place the potato chips on the towel. Heat for 30 seconds. Repeat if necessary. The towel absorbs excess moisture from the potato chips, restoring the crispness to the chips.

- **Revive Stale Bread.** Dampen a dish towel with water, cover the loaf of bread, and place it in the microwave oven. Heat for 10 seconds, infusing the bread with steam. Repeat if necessary until the bread feels adequately rehydrated.

How to Clean Oven Racks with Ammonia

WHAT YOU NEED

- Paper towels
- Large plastic trash bag
- Measuring cup
- 1 cup of ammonia
- Twist tie
- Garden hose
- Dishwashing liquid
- Water
- Dish towel

WHAT TO DO

1. Bring the oven rack outside, and wrap paper towels around it.
2. Place the rack inside a large plastic trash bag.
3. Carefully saturate the paper towels with 1 cup of ammonia—without breathing in the ammonia.
4. Close the bag securely with a twist tie.
5. Let the bag sit overnight outside or in a well-ventilated garage.
6. The next morning, open the bag outdoors (again being careful to avoid breathing the fumes).
7. Remove the rack, leaving the paper towels in the bag.
8. Discard the bag.
9. Rinse the rack with a garden hose.
10. Bring the oven rack inside the house and wash it thoroughly with soapy water. Rinse clean and dry with a dish towel.

HOW IT WORKS

The ammonia fumes loosen the baked-on food and grease from the oven racks.

HOT DIGGETY

Another way to clean excessive baked-on food and grease from an oven rack: place an old towel on the floor of the bathtub, fill the tub with enough hot water to cover the racks, add 1 cup of liquid laundry detergent, and let sit for 1 hour. Wipe the racks clean with a sponge and rinse.

How to Kill Mold in a Refrigerator Drip Tray with Mouthwash

WHAT YOU NEED

- Sponge
- Water
- Dishwashing liquid
- Measuring cup
- 1 cup of Listerine antiseptic mouthwash
- Soft, clean dish towel

WHAT TO DO

1. Remove the tray from underneath the refrigerator and, using a sponge, wash it with soapy water made with dishwashing liquid, and rinse clean.
2. Sit the drip tray on the counter, add 1 cup of Listerine antiseptic mouthwash, and fill the rest of the drip tray with water.
3. Let the solution in the drip tray sit undisturbed for 1 hour.
4. Rinse the drip tray clean and dry with a soft, clean dish towel.
5. Return the drip tray to its proper place beneath the refrigerator.

HOW IT WORKS

Listerine mouthwash, originally invented in the nineteenth century as an antiseptic for use during surgery to kill germs, kills mold and mildew.

DON'T BE SUCH A DRIP

- Condensation builds up in refrigerator and freezer compartments. To prevent frost from building up inside the appliance, these water droplets drain through tubes into a drip pan underneath the refrigerator, where heat from the condenser causes it to evaporate.
- The drip pan should be cleaned regularly to eliminate the potential of mold and bacterial growth. Aside from causing health dangers, mold can produce an unpleasant smell.
- Another way to kill mold in a refrigerator drip tray: remove the tray, fill it with water, add 1 tablespoon of borax, and scrub. Rinse well, dry with a cloth, and replace the tray.

More Things to Store in the Refrigerator

- **Nail Polish.** Storing nail polish in the refrigerator will extend its life, provided you leave the polish in the refrigerator for several weeks. The cool temperature slows the thickening agents and reduces solvent evaporation. Allow the  nail polish to return to room temperature before using, otherwise water condensation inside the bottle will taint the polish.

- **Panty Hose.** To prolong the life of panty hose and prevent runs, dampen a new pair of panty hose with water, wring them out, place them inside a resealable plastic bag, and seal shut. Place the bag in the freezer. When you're ready to wear the panty hose, defrost, and let them dry.

- **Sealed Envelope.** If you need to reopen a sealed envelope to add something else to the letter, place the envelope inside a resealable storage bag, seal it shut, and place in the freezer for 2 hours. Use a letter opener to snap open the adhesive strip. Let the envelope return to room temperature and seal it shut again.

- **Sheets.** To kill dust mites living in sheets, place your sheets in a plastic trash bag and place it in the freezer overnight. The next morning, wash the sheets. The freezing temperatures kill the dust mites.

- **Superglue.** According to the Super Glue Corporation, superglue lasts longest when stored upright in dry, cool conditions like a refrigerator.

4

FRUITS, VEGETABLES, AND GRAINS

While using a sharp chef's knife to cut a large acorn squash in half, I nearly disembowled myself—rather than the gourd.

"This is like trying to cut through cement," I told my wife, Debbie, which gave me a mischevious idea.

I carried the acorn squash outside to our backyard, held it at shoulder height, and dropped it on the concrete patio.

With a resounding thud, the gourd boke into four convenient pieces.

I brought them back into the kitchen, and with a self-satisfied grin on my face, scooped out the innnards.

"Better you than me," I told the gourd.

How to Prevent Sliced Apples from Browning with Salt

WHAT YOU NEED

- Measuring spoons
- ¼ teaspoon of salt
- Measuring cup
- 2 cups of cold water
- Paper towel

WHAT TO DO

1. Dissolve ¼ teaspoon of salt in 2 cups of cold water.
2. Immerse the apple slices in the saltwater solution and lay a sheet of paper towel on top to prevent the slices from floating to the top. Let the apple slices sit in the salty water for 10 minutes.
3. Drain the apples from the salt water.
4. Rinse the apples in fresh water to remove excess salt.

HOW IT WORKS

Sliced apples tend to brown quickly when exposed to air. Apples contain the enzyme polyphenol oxidase. When an apple is sliced open, oxygen in the air causes the polyphenol oxidase enzymes to oxidize phenolic compounds in the apple tissue, eventually producing melanins: brown pigments. Soaking the sliced apples in salty water blocks the oxygen in the air from reaching the polyphenol oxidase enzymes and triggering the reaction.

TRUE COLORS

- Some apples seem to brown faster than others because the concentration of phenolic compounds differs between varieties of apples, such as McIntosh, Granny Smith, and Red Delicious. Also, the concentration of phenolic compounds depends on growing conditions and the age of the fruit.
- Aside from soaking apple slices in salt water, coating freshly cut apples in sugar or syrup can reduce oxygen diffusion and slow the browning reaction.
- Coating apple slices with lemon or pineapple juice, both of which contain antioxidants, slows enzymatic browning. Additionally, the acidity

of lemon and pineapple juice lowers the pH of the apple, slowing the polyphenol oxidase.

- Blanching sliced apples in boiling water for 4 to 5 minutes deactivates the polyphenol oxides, virtually halting any browning.

EVERY TRICK IN THE BOOK
Salt of the Earth

You can also use salt to:

- **Flavor Watermelon.** Sprinkling watermelon with salt gives the fruit a unique taste.
- **Extend the Shelf Life of Milk and Cream and Prevent Spoilage.** Add a pinch of salt to the milk or cream.
- **Improve the Efficiency of a Double Boiler.** Dissolve 1 teaspoon of salt in the water in the bottom half of the double boiler. The salt raises the boiling point of water, transmitting more heat to the food in the upper half of the boiler.
- **Clean a Wet Spill from Inside an Oven.** Immediately and carefully cover the spill with salt. When the oven cools down, scrape up the mess.
- **Purge Insects from Broccoli, Brussels Sprouts, Cabbage, or Cauliflower.** Dissolve 2 tablespoons of salt in 1 quart of cold water, soak the broccoli, brussels sprouts, cabbage, or cauliflower in the solution for 15 minutes, and rinse clean.
- **Prevent Fish from Sticking to a Frying Pan.** Sprinkle a little salt in the skillet before frying.
- **Make Peeling Potatoes a Snap.** Dissolve ½ cup of salt in 1 gallon of water, and soak the potatoes in the salt water for 30 minutes before peeling.
- **Remove Sand from Spinach.** Mix 2 tablespoons of salt per 1 cup of water, and wash the spinach in the salty solution. The salt water removes the sand with just one washing.

How to Rescue Mushy Beans with Sour Cream

WHAT YOU NEED

- Potato masher
- Stove
- Large plate
- Spatula
- Grated pita bread, raw vegetables, or tortilla chips

For each cup of beans:

- 1 tablespoon of minced garlic
- 1 tablespoon of olive oil
- 1 cup of sour cream
- 1 cup of ripe olives, chopped
- 1 cup of onion, chopped
- 2 cups of cheddar cheese, grated

WHAT TO DO

1. If you overcook beans, turning them into unrecognizable glop, leave the beans in the pot or saucepan and add 1 tablespoon of minced garlic and 1 tablespoon of olive oil per each cup of beans.

2. Use a potato masher to mash the beans over a medium heat on the stove just long enough for the beans to break up and come together into a paste without liquefying.

3. Spread the beans on a large plate.

4. Using a spatula, spread the sour cream over beans.

5. Layer the olives, chopped onion, and cheese over the sour cream and beans.

6. Serve with wedges of pita bread, raw vegetables, or tortilla chips.

HOW IT WORKS

Mashing up the beans and heating them into a paste creates refried beans. The sour cream adds moisture to the dish, and the spices, chopped onion, and cheese add flavor.

SPILLING THE BEANS

- You can also salvage mushy beans by pouring them into a blender and pureeing, turning them into bean soup.
- Store dried beans in an airtight container in a cool place. Temperatures above 100° Fahrenheit cause chemical changes in the beans to the extent that they can no longer be softened.
- Contrary to popular belief, soaking beans in salted water does not hinder beans from softening. In actuality, soaking beans for 2 hours in a solution of 1 tablespoon of salt dissolved in 1 gallon of water enables the softening process.
- Soaking or cooking beans in hard water (with high mineral content) prevents softening. The calcium and magnesium in the hard water form insoluble compounds in the cell walls of the beans. Adding a pinch of baking soda to the water removes the calcium and magnesium from the water. Adding too much baking soda, however, softens the beans excessively, turning them into bland mush.

- To soften dried beans, cover the beans with boiling water and let sit for 1 hour before cooking. Adding a pinch of baking soda to the solution speeds up the process. The alkaline sodium bicarbonate breaks down the fibrous cellulose skins, making them more permeable to water.
- To cook dried beans, simmer the softened beans over low heat to avoid boiling over and stir occasionally and gently with a wooden spoon to avoid breaking the skins.

EVERY TRICK IN THE BOOK
Sour Power

You can also use sour cream to:

- **Substitute for Cream Cheese.** Sour cream makes an excellent creamy spread on bagels or toast.
- **Make a Flakier Piecrust.** Substitute sour cream for the liquid called for in the recipe.
- **Prevent Grated Potatoes from Discoloring.** Mix the potatoes with a teaspoon or two of sour cream.
- **Adorn Soups.** Swirl a spoonful of sour cream into borscht or any creamy vegetable soups.

- **Garnish Vegetables.** Add a dollop of sour cream to any sweet roasted vegetable for a creamy embellishment.
- **Thicken Vinaigrette Salad Dressings.** Add 1 teaspoon of sour cream to thicken up any vinaigrette. Shake well.
- **Garnish Pancakes, Crepes, and Blintzes.** For a more flavorful taste than butter, spread sour cream on your pancakes, crepes, and blintzes.

How to Cook Asparagus with Panty Hose

WHAT YOU NEED

- Scissors
- Clean, used pair of panty hose
- Pot with lid
- Stove
- Tongs
- Paper towel

WHAT TO DO

1. Using a pair of scissors, carefully cut strips from the leg of a clean pair of panty hose. Each strip should be approximately 6 inches long and 1 inch wide.
2. Tie the asparagus spears together in bundles of 10 with a strip of panty hose.
3. Fill a pot with water and bring it to a boil. Lower the heat to medium.
4. Stand the bundles of asparagus in the pot of gently boiling water with the tips just above the water level.

5. Cover with a lid for 12 minutes, allowing the boiling water to cook the stems while the steam softens the tips.
6. Using tongs, carefully remove the bundles of asparagus from the boiling water.
7. Untie the panty hose strips.
8. Roll the stalks quickly in a sheet of paper towel to remove all the water, and serve.

HOW IT WORKS

They nylon panty hose strip allows you to remove the asparagus spears easily from the water without breaking off the tips.

ASPARAGUS TIPS

- To trim asparagus spears to the top 4 or 5 inches, hold one spear with both hands and bend it until it snaps naturally at the spot where it becomes tough, leaving only the tender end of the spear.
- To keep trimmed asparagus fresh before cooking, fill a tall drinking glass with 1 inch of ice water, and stand the asparagus stalks upright in the glass. Cover with a resealable plastic bag, place in the refrigerator for up to 1 hour, and then cook as usual.
- To revitalize wilted asparagus, use a knife to slice 1 inch from the bottom of each spear, mix 1 teaspoon of lemon juice and 2 quarts of cool water in a mixing bowl or pot, and soak the asparagus in the solution for 30 minutes to 1 hour.

How to Rescue Overcooked Vegetables with Chicken or Beef Broth

WHAT YOU NEED

- Pot or saucepan
- Potato masher
- Measuring cup
- ½ cup chicken or beef broth
- ¼ teaspoon of parsley, chopped fine
- ¼ teaspoon of tarragon, chopped fine
- ¼ teaspoon of thyme, chopped fine
- ¼ teaspoon of garlic powder
- Stove
- Ice cube tray
- Resealable freezer bag

WHAT TO DO

1. Place the overcooked vegetables in a pot or saucepan.
2. Using the potato masher, mash up the vegetables.
3. Add ½ cup of chicken or beef broth (or enough to make a thick bouillon).

4. Add the parsley, tarragon, thyme, and garlic powder.
5. Over medium heat, stir well.
6. Pour the mixture into the compartments of the ice cube tray.
7. Place the ice cube tray in the freezer.
8. After the cubes freeze solid, pop the vegetable bouillon cubes from the tray, and place them in a resealable freezer bag.
9. Whenever cooking soup, add a few bouillon cubes to the pot to enhance the flavor.

HOW IT WORKS

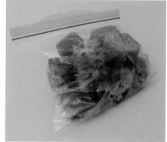

Mashing the vegetables, adding broth and herbs, and freezing the result in an ice cube tray creates flavorful vegetable bouillon cubes.

GETTING OUT OF A MESS

You can also turn overcooked vegetables into:

- **Baby Food.** Puree the soggy vegetables in a blender. Pour into airtight containers and freeze.
- **Vegetable Casserole.** For every 2 cups of overcooked vegetables, add 1 beaten egg and ¼ cup of bread crumbs. Pour the mixture into a casserole dish, top with ¼ cup of shredded cheese, and bake for approximately 15 minutes.
- **Vegetable Parmesan.** Toss the mushy vegetables in cold water to stop the cooking process, and drain. Sprinkle with pepper, and top with shaved Parmesan cheese and bread crumbs.

EVERY TRICK IN THE BOOK

Too Many Cooks

You can also use broth to:

- **Prevent the Fat from Burning on a Roasting Chicken or Turkey.** Baste the bird with ¼ cup of chicken broth.
- **Enhance the Taste of Artichokes.** Cooking artichokes in any flavor broth makes artichokes far tastier than cooking them in water.
- **Cook Up Flavorful Rice.** Place the rice in a short, wide pot, add two parts boiling chicken broth to one part rice, cover immediately with a lid that fits tightly, and set the pot over low heat on the stove undisturbed until the rice absorbs all the broth.
- **Give Lima Beans a Wonderful Flavor.** Steam the beans in chicken broth.
- **Enhance the Flavor of Poached Eggs.** Substitute chicken broth for the water.
- **Tenderize a Pot Roast.** Add equal parts strong brewed tea and beef broth to a tough pot roast. The tannic acid in tea is a natural meat tenderizer.

How to Pit Cherries with a Chopstick

WHAT YOU NEED

- Clean, empty wine bottle
- 1 chopstick

WHAT TO DO

1. Set a cherry upright on the mouth of the wine bottle and hold the fruit in place with your fingers.
2. Pluck off the stem.
3. Press the wide end of the chopstick into the dimple left by the cherry stem, pushing the pit through the bottom of the cherry and into the wine bottle.

HOW IT WORKS

The mouth of the bottle provides the proper rim to hold the cherry in place, the chopstick is just the right width to push the pit out of the cherry, and the bottle collects all the pits.

A BOWL OF CHERRIES

- To prevent cherry juice splatters when using the above method, place the wine bottle inside a paper grocery bag to contain the splashes.
- For another effective way to remove the pit from cherries, use a large hairpin or knitting needle.
- Remove cherries from the refrigerator 1 hour before serving to allow the fruit to thaw to room temperature for the best taste.

- To freeze cherries, rinse well, pat dry with a paper towel, and pit. Place the prepared cherries inside a resealable plastic bag, and store in the freezer for up to 1 year.
- Remove cherry stains from your hands with lemon juice or by rubbing your skin with a cut lemon.

EVERY TRICK IN THE BOOK
Chop Chop!

You can also use chopsticks to:

- **Clear a Funnel.** Use a chopstick to push syrupy liquids through the hole in a funnel.
- **Create Knitting Needles.** Sharpen the ends of two chopsticks with a pencil sharpener, smooth the points with fine sandpaper, and give the raw wood a glossy coat by rubbing it with waxed paper.
- **Dry Plastic Bags.** Place a few chopsticks in a jar, and after washing the plastic bags with soapy water, hang them upside down on the sticks to dry.
- **Hold Up a Hair Bun.** Use chopsticks as hair sticks.
- **Label Potted Plants with Care Instructions.** Write the instructions for the proper care of a plant on an index card or seed packet, tape it to the thick end of a chopstick, and push the sharp end of the stick into the soil in the plant's pot.
- **Level Off Measured Dry Ingredients.** Fill a measuring cup with the dry ingredient, and glide the chopstick across the rims of the measuring cup to level it off.
- **Make Homemade Popsicles.** Fill a drinking glass with lemonade, insert a chopstick, and freeze.
- **Stir a Cocktail.** A chopstick makes an excellent swizzle stick.
- **Toast Marshmallows.** Poke a marshmallow onto the end of a chopstick and hold it over a fire.
- **Whisk Eggs.** Use two chopsticks, held together, to beat the eggs in a bowl.

How to Shuck an Ear of Corn with a Paper Towel

WHAT YOU NEED
- Paper towel
- Water

WHAT TO DO
1. Shuck the husk from the ear of corn.
2. Dampen a sheet of paper towel with water.
3. With the damp sheet of paper towel, wipe the exposed ear of corn in a single stroke from top to bottom.

HOW IT WORKS
The paper towel removes the silk from the ear of corn.

AW, SHUCKS!
- You can also detach the silk from a shucked ear of corn by rubbing the ear with a balled-up clean, used pair of panty hose.
- Remove stubborn corn silk with a toothbrush dampened with water. Simply hold the end of the stalk and bush downward toward the end of the cob.

- To strip whole kernels of corn from the cob, dip the ear in boiling water for 1 or 2 minutes and cool under cold running water. Doing so prevents the milk inside the kernels from spurting when you strip them off with a knife.
- Before boiling corn on the cob, use the green leaves from the corn to line the bottom of the pot of water. Boiling the cob with the leaves enhances the taste of the corn.

How to Revitalize Wilted Lettuce with Lemon Juice

WHAT YOU NEED

- 2 large bowls
- Cold water
- Measuring spoons
- 2 tablespoons of lemon juice
- Refrigerator
- Ice water
- 1 tablespoon of apple cider vinegar
- Plate
- Hot water

WHAT TO DO

1. Fill a large bowl halfway with cold water.
2. Add 2 tablespoons of lemon juice and stir well.
3. Remove any browned leaves from the head of lettuce.
4. Place the lettuce in the bowl and refrigerate for 1 hour.

5. Before removing the bowl of lettuce from the refrigerator, fill another large bowl halfway with ice water.

6. Add 1 tablespoon of apple cider vinegar to the bowl of ice water, and mix well.

7. Remove the bowl containing the lettuce from the refrigerator, remove the head of lettuce, and place it on a plate.

8. Discard the lemony water, and fill the bowl with hot water.

9. Douse the head of lettuce quickly in the bowl of hot water.

10. Immediately immerse the head of lettuce in the prepared bowl of ice water.

HOW IT WORKS

As lettuce loses moisture in the refrigerator due to evaporation, the leaves begin to wilt and droop. Soaking the lettuce in water rehydrates the leaves, replacing the water in the cells through osmosis. Adding lemon juice boosts the hydration process. The citric acid in the vinegar encourages cell turnover within the leaves, making them absorb more water.

DON'T LET LETTUCE UPSET US

- To keep washed or revived lettuce crisp for as long as possible, dry it thoroughly and then wrap the head of lettuce in a sheet of paper towel, place it inside a plastic bag, and seal tightly. The paper towel absorbs the excess moisture on the leaves, hindering bacteria growth.

- Kathleen M. Brown, professor of plant stress biology at Penn State University, disputes the need for lemon juice. "Additives actually reduce the difference in osmotic potential between the vegetable and water and reduce the rehydration rate," she told the *Washington Post*.

- If the lettuce changes color, is covered with dark spots, becomes slimy, or generates bacterial or mold growth, discard it.

How to Avoid Crying When Cutting Onions with a Swimming Mask

WHAT YOU NEED

- Rubber kitchen gloves
- Snorkel
- Swimming mask or goggles
- Sharp knife
- Onions
- Cutting board

WHAT TO DO

1. Put on a pair of rubber kitchen gloves.
2. To make sure the swimming mask will fit comfortably, hold the mask up to your face—without placing the strap around your head—and inhale quickly with your nose, sucking air from inside the mask so the rubber gasket forms a tight seal against your face.
3. With the snorkel attached to the rubber strap, place a swimming mask or goggles over your eyes with the strap securely over your head.
4. Insert the mouthpiece of the snorkel in your mouth and breathe normally through the tube.
5. Using the knife, carefully slice the onions on the cutting board.

HOW IT WORKS

Wearing rubber kitchen gloves keep onion odor off your hands. Wearing a swimming mask while cutting onions prevents the chemical irritant syn-propanethial S-oxide, produced as a vapor when you cut into an onion, from coming into contact with your eyes and irritating the lachrymal glands, which respond by producing the tears. The snorkel isn't really necessary. It just makes you look more committed (or like someone who should be committed).

KNOW YOUR ONIONS

Other ways to avoid tears when cutting an onion:

- Before cutting the onions, refrigerate them for at least 1 hour (or freeze for 30 minutes). The cold slows down the reaction rate of the enzymes that create the chemical irritant.
- Place a cutting board in a wide, flat dish or pan, fill with pan with cold water, and carefully slice the onion underwater. The water prevents the sulfuric compounds from reaching your eyes and inducing tears.
- Running an exhaust fan or a desk fan while chopping onions helps remove the tear-inducing vapors from the room.
- If you light a candle and place it next to your cutting board, the flame will burn off the sulfuric compounds before the vapor can reach your eyes.

EVERY TRICK IN THE BOOK

More Onion Feats

You can also use onions to:

- **Make French-Fried Onion Rings.** Prepare the batter for any pan-cake mix in a bowl, dry the onion rings on a sheet of paper towel, dip the dry rings in the batter, and fry briskly in a buttered pan.

- **Sweeten Strong Onions.** Slice and separate the onion into rings, mix 1 teaspoon of white vinegar in a bowl of cold water, and soak the onion rings in the solution for 30 minutes. Rinse with cool water, and dry with a paper towel.
- **Preserve Half an Onion.** If you only need to use half of an onion, rub the open face of the leftover half with butter to seal it, place it in a resealable plastic bag, and refrigerate.
- **Protect Other Foods from Onions.** If storing whole onions in the refrigerator, wrap each onion in a sheet of aluminum foil to prevent its strong odor from tainting the flavor and smell of other foods in the vegetable crisper. Do not store whole onions in a plastic bag.
- **Enhance the Taste of Sautéed Onions.** Before sautéing onions in butter, add a little honey to the butter.
- **Improve the Taste of a Stew or Casserole.** Before adding sliced onion to a stew or casserole, sauté the onions lightly in olive oil.

How to Speed Up a Baked Potato with a Carpenter's Nail

WHAT YOU NEED

- One long, heavy nail, 3½ inches in length
- Cupcake or muffin tin
- Measuring cup
- Water
- Fork (optional)
- Oven
- Oven mitt
- Knife

WHAT TO DO

1. Insert a long, heavy nail lengthwise through the potato.
2. Place the potato in a cupcake or muffin tin.
3. Using a measuring cup, fill any empty compartments with water to prevent the cupcake or muffin tin from smoking.

4. If you prefer dry baked potatoes, use the tines of a fork to prick both ends of the potato before baking to allow the steam to escape.

5. Bake the potato in a standard oven (not a microwave oven) at 400° Fahrenheit for approximately 35 minutes. (A metal nail in a *microwave* oven will heat up, causing the metal to ignite, setting fire to the potato and destroying the microwave oven.)

6. Wearing an oven mitt, carefully remove the baked potato from the oven.

7. To prevent a freshly baked potato from getting too soggy on the inside, cut into the baked potato with a knife to let the steam to escape.

HOW IT WORKS

The nail transfers the heat produced by the oven to the center of the potato, reducing baking time by approximately 15 minutes.

HOT POTATO

- Without a nail inserted into the potato, a medium to large potato takes 50 to 60 minutes to bake in a standard oven at 400° Fahrenheit.

- Rubbing butter over the skins of the potatoes before baking prevents the skins from cracking and improves the taste of the potatoes.

- If you wrap a potato in aluminum foil and bake it in a standard oven, the potato will taste steamed rather than baked.

- Adding potatoes to a pan of roasted meat roughly 40 minutes before the meat is done allows the potatoes to bake and absorb the meat flavor.

- To bake a potato in a microwave oven, pierce the skin with the tines of a fork to create vent holes for the steam to escape as the potato cooks. Otherwise, the potato may explode in the microwave oven.

- To reheat a leftover baked potato, dip it in hot water, and then warm in the microwave oven for 1 to 2 minutes.

How to Fix Soggy Mashed Potatoes with Powdered Milk

WHAT YOU NEED
- Measuring spoons
- 1 tablespoon powdered milk
- Whisk
- Stove

WHAT TO DO
1. Leaving the mashed potatoes in the pot, sprinkle 1 tablespoon of powdered milk into the mashed potatoes.
2. Whisk well over low heat until the mashed potatoes become fluffy.
3. If the mashed potatoes remain soggy, repeat steps 1 and 2 above as many times as necessary.

HOW IT WORKS
Adding milk to overcooked mashed potatoes usually makes them soggier. Adding powdered milk adds no liquid to the potatoes. Instead, the excess moisture in the mashed potatoes rehydrates the powdered milk, giving the potatoes a creamy taste.

SMALL POTATOES
- After draining boiled potatoes to be mashed, set a blow-dryer on warm, and blow the wet potatoes until they dry. Dry potatoes produce creamier mashed potatoes.

- Another way to fix soggy mashed potatoes: Let the potatoes cool to room temperature, add some minced onion, 2 beaten egg yolks, and some salt. Form into patties, fry in a pan greased with vegetable oil, and serve potato latkes.
- When mashing potatoes, add a pinch of baking powder (not baking soda) for each potato. When heated, the baking powder will produce small air pockets in the mashed potatoes, making them fluffier.
- To improve the appearance and taste of mashed potatoes, beat an egg in a bowl with a whisk, pour it into the potatoes, and blend well.

- Make colorful mashed potatoes to enliven any special occasion by blending a few drops of food coloring into the cooked mashed potatoes.

EVERY TRICK IN THE BOOK
Keep Your Powder Dry

You can also use powdered milk to:

- **Bake a Loaf of Bread with a Shiny Crust.** Whisk 1 egg in a bowl, add 1 teaspoon of powdered milk and 1 tablespoon of water, and blend well. Before putting the bread in the oven, use a pastry brush to paint the solution on the top of the loaf.
- **Keep Cauliflower Bright White.** Add 1 tablespoon of powdered milk to the cooking water.
- **Flavor Corn on the Cob Without Using Sugar or Salt.** Sprinkle 1 teaspoon of powdered milk into the water when boiling corn on the cob.

- **Make Whipped Topping.** Add equal parts powdered milk and ice water to a mixing bowl, and whip with an electric mixer at the highest speed for 3 or 4 minutes (or until the topping stands up in peaks). Add a few drops of vanilla extract and beat again. Add sugar to taste and beat once more.
- **Create a Crisp, Flaky Pastry.** Add 1 tablespoon of powdered milk to the flour, use ice-cold water whenever the recipe calls for water, and add ½ tablespoon of lemon juice to the dough.

How to Turn Soggy Rice into Fried Rice with an Egg

WHAT YOU NEED

- Refrigerator
- 2 cups of soggy rice
- 2 eggs
- Bowl
- Saucepan
- Stove
- Measuring spoons
- 1 tablespoon of vegetable oil
- Wooden spoon
- 1 small onion, diced
- ¼ red bell pepper, diced
- ¼ cup of frozen peas, defrosted
- Soy sauce

WHAT TO DO

1. Refrigerate the rice overnight to dry out the soggy rice.
2. Use your fingers to break up the clumps of rice into individual grains.
3. Beat 2 eggs in a bowl.
4. In the saucepan, heat 1 tablespoon of vegetable oil on high heat.
5. Add the diced onion and bell pepper, and fry for 1 to 2 minutes.
6. Add the rice and fry for 2 minutes, stirring throughout and breaking up any clumps in the rice.
7. Pour the eggs over the rice, and fry for about 1 minute or until all rice is coated with egg.
8. Add the peas and fry continuously for another minute.

9. When steam rises from the rice, the dish is ready.

10. Add soy sauce to taste.

HOW IT WORKS

Placing the soggy rice in the refrigerator overnight desiccates the excess moisture from the grain, and coating the rice with egg seals in the remaining moisture and—along with the onion, pepper, and peas—gives the rice a zesty flavor.

ALL WET

You can also use soggy rice to make:

- **Rice Meatballs.** Mix the soggy rice with an equal amount of minced meat. The rice fills the meatballs, stretching the meat, without sacrificing any flavor.

- **Rice Pancakes.** Pre-heat a nonstick skillet over medium-high heat. In a mixing bowl, combine 1½ cups of soggy rice, 1 large egg, ½ teaspoon of vanilla extract, ½ teaspoon of cinnamon, and ¼ teaspoon of salt. Using an  ice cream scooper, put ⅓ cup of the rice mixture onto the skillet. Using a spatula, flatten the rice ball into a pancake roughly ½ inch thick. Repeat until the skillet is full. Fry for roughly 5 minutes, flip the pancakes, and fry for another 5 minutes. When golden brown on both sides, serve.

- **Rice Porridge.** In a clean, medium saucepan, mix 3 cups of soggy rice, 1¾ cups of milk, 3 tablespoons of brown sugar, 2 tablespoons of raisins, ¾ teaspoon of ground cinnamon, and a pinch of salt. Bring to a boil over medium heat. Turn down the heat and, stirring often, cook until thickened to your preference. Remove from heat, and stir in ¾ teaspoon of vanilla extract.

How to Turn Soggy Rice into Rice Pudding with Milk

WHAT YOU NEED

- Clean, medium saucepan
- Measuring cup
- Measuring spoons
- 1½ cups of soggy rice
- 2 cups of milk
- ⅓ cup of sugar
- ¼ teaspoon of salt
- 1 egg, beaten
- Wooden spoon
- Stove
- ⅔ cup of raisins
- 1 tablespoon of butter
- ½ teaspoon of vanilla extract

WHAT TO DO

1. In a clean, medium saucepan, combine 1½ cups of soggy rice, 1½ cups of milk, ⅓ cup of sugar, ¼ teaspoon of salt, and 1 beaten egg.
2. Using a wooden spoon, mix the ingredients in the saucepan thoroughly.
3. Cook on the stove over medium heat until thick and creamy (usually 25 to 35 minutes), stirring frequently to keep the ingredients evenly distributed.
4. Stir in an additional ½ cup of milk and ⅔ cup of raisins.
5. Cook for another 3 to 5 minutes, stirring constantly.
6. Remove from heat, and stir in 1 tablespoon of butter and ½ teaspoon of vanilla extract.
7. Serve.

HOW IT WORKS

Soggy rice is essentially the main ingredient in any recipe for rice pudding.

RICE IS NICE

- To cook rice properly, add three parts boiling water for every two parts rice in a short, wide pot, and bring the uncovered pot to a boil. Turn down the heat, cover immediately with a lid that fits tightly, and set the pot over low, undisturbed, until the rice absorbs all the water.

- To salvage burned rice, remove the pot from the stove, place a slice of white bread on top of the rice, and cover the pot with the lid. Let the rice sit undisturbed for a few minutes. Then open the lid, remove the slice of bread, and discard it. The bread absorbs the burned flavor.

- Keep cooked rice warm without turning it sticky by covering the mouth of the pot with a few sheets of paper towel and placing the lid over it. The paper towel absorbs the steam that typically condenses into water droplets under the lid, stopping it from dripping and turning the rice sticky.

- To cook up chicken-flavored rice, place the uncooked rice in a pot, add two parts chicken broth for every one part rice, and bring to a boil. Reduce the heat, cover tightly with a snug lid, and simmer for approximately 15 minutes or until the rice absorbs all the broth.

- Make white rice appear buttered by adding a few drops of yellow food coloring to the boiling water before tossing in the rice.

- To prevent rice from sticking to the inside of the pot, spray the inside of the pot with vegetable cooking spray before adding the water and rice.

- Adding 1 teaspoon of lemon juice for each quart of water before cooking rice yields the whitest, fluffiest rice—with a lemony flavor. The lemon juice also helps prevent the finished rice from sticking together.

- Adding 1 teaspoon of vegetable oil to the water in the pot before adding the rice helps prevent the rice from boiling over.

EVERY TRICK IN THE BOOK
Against the Grain

You can also use rice to:

- **Prevent Scalloped Potatoes from Curdling.** Use ½ cup of rice for thickening.
- **Relieve Heartburn.** Eating rice, a food high in complex carbohydrates, absorbs acid in the stomach, relieving heartburn.
- **Make a Heating Pad.** See page 192.
- **Prevent Salt from Clumping Together in a Salt Shaker.** Add a few grains of rice to the salt shaker. The rice absorbs the moisture that would otherwise cause the salt to clump together. Replace the rice once a year.
- **Clean the Inside of a Vase, Glass Bottle, Water Bottle, or Thermos Bottle.** Pour 2 tablespoons of uncooked rice into the vase or bottle and add ½ cup of white vinegar. Shake vigorously, and then rinse clean. Repeat if necessary.

How to Reheat Leftover Rice with an Ice Cube

WHAT YOU NEED

- Microwave-safe bowl
- Ice cube
- Plastic wrap
- Fork
- Microwave oven

WHAT TO DO

1. To reheat cool or leftover rice, place the rice in a microwave-safe bowl.
2. Place an ice cube on top of the rice.
3. Cover the bowl with a sheet of plastic wrap.
4. Use the tines of a fork to perforate a few holes in the center of the plastic so steam can escape when you heat up the rice in the microwave oven.
5. For every 1 cup of rice in the bowl, heat in the microwave oven for 90 seconds and add another ice cube.

HOW IT WORKS

As the microwave oven reheats the rice, the ice cube melts, adding vital moisture to the rice.

THE PRICE OF RICE

A few other methods to reheat leftover rice stored in the freezer or refrigerator:

- Cover the rice with boiling water, let sit for 3 minutes, and drain.
- Place the rice in a baking dish and sprinkle with 1 or 2 teaspoons of water, drizzle with olive oil to prevent sticking and add flavor (if desired), and cover with a lid (or with aluminum foil, sealed tightly). Bake at 300° Fahrenheit for approximately 15 minutes or until the rice is warm. Remove from the oven, and fluff with a fork.
- Pour the rice into a pot, break up any clumps with a wooden spoon, sprinkle with 3 tablespoons of water, and heat on the stove over medium heat, stirring occasionally to prevent scorching. When you hear the water boiling and see steam start to rise, reduce the heat to the lowest setting, cover, and let steam for 3 to 5 minutes, stirring once or twice. Remove from the heat, and fluff with a fork.

How to Remove Stems from Strawberries with a Drinking Straw

WHAT YOU NEED
- Sink
- Water
- Plastic drinking straw

WHAT TO DO
1. Do not remove the stems from strawberries or slice them until after you wash them. Hulled and sliced strawberries absorb water and become soggy, losing their flavor.
2. Fill the sink halfway with water and toss in the strawberries. The strawberries will float on the surface.
3. Use the spray attachment to spray the strawberries with cold water and make them tumble. Dirt, grit, and sand will sink to the bottom.
4. Pluck out the strawberries, drain the sink, and repeat if necessary.
5. Fluff up the stem of a single strawberry.
6. Place your thumb over one end of a plastic drinking straw to cover the hole.
7. Push the other end of the plastic drinking straw through the middle bottom of the strawberry.
8. Continue pushing the straw through the strawberry toward the stem until it pops off.
9. Remove the straw.

HOW IT WORKS
The entire strawberry stem will poke through the top in one piece.

STRAWBERRY FIELDS FOREVER
- To freeze clean, hulled strawberries, spread the berries on a cookie sheet, cover with plastic wrap, and place in the freezer until they freeze solid. Then place the frozen berries in a resealable freezer bag, remove as much air as possible, seal securely, write the date on the bag with an indelible marker, and freeze. The strawberries will last up to 6 months.
- Sprinkling sugar over strawberries softens the strawberries. Do so only immediately before serving.
- To cut strawberries into uniform slices quickly and efficiently, use an egg slicer.

How to Peel Tomatoes with Panty Hose

WHAT YOU NEED

- Scissors
- Clean, used pair of panty hose
- Sharp knife
- Red, ripe tomatoes
- Reusable plastic kitchen gloves
- Pot
- Boiling water
- 2 large bowls
- Ice water

WHAT TO DO

1. To peel many tomatoes at once, use a pair of scissors to cut off one of the legs from a clean, used pair of panty hose.
2. With the sharp knife, cut a small, shallow X in the bottom of each tomato.
3. Place the tomatoes inside the nylon panty hose leg.
4. Wearing reusable plastic kitchen gloves, carefully submerge the filled stocking into a pot of boiling water for 1 minute.
5. Remove the panty hose leg filled with tomatoes from the water, and plunge it into a bowl of ice water to stop the cooking.
6. Remove the tomato-filled panty hose leg from the ice water, and empty the tomatoes into a bowl.
7. Using the knife and starting at the X on the bottom of the tomato, slide the skin off each tomato.

HOW IT WORKS

The boiling water separates the tomato skin from the pulp.

HOT TOMATOES

- Another trick to peel a firm tomato: gently rub the entire tomato skin with a wooden spoon (loosening the skin from the pulp), split the skin with a knife, and peel.

5

DAIRY AND EGGS

Whenever I grate cheese, I wear a metal thimble on each finger. Sure, I look a bit silly, but I'd rather grate the cheese than my fingertips.

Wearing the thimbles also allows me to grate faster and more thoroughly, shredding the entire block of cheese.

I also hold the grater inside a large resealable plastic bag and grate the cheese inside the bag. That way, the grated cheese drops into the bag rather than making a mess all over the kitchen counter.

The thimbles will also come in handy if I ever decide to play an old-fashioned washboard in a Kentucky bluegrass band.

Or darn my socks.

How to Make a Cream Cheese Substitute with Yogurt

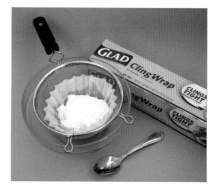

WHAT YOU NEED

- Paper coffee filter
- Small metal strainer
- Bowl
- 1 cup of plain yogurt
- Plastic wrap
- Refrigerator
- Spoon
- Airtight container

WHAT TO DO

1. Place a paper coffee filter inside a small metal strainer.
2. Sit the lined strainer inside a bowl.
3. Fill the coffee filter with 1 cup of plain yogurt.
4. Cover the strainer and bowl with a sheet of plastic wrap and refrigerate overnight (for a minimum of 8 hours).
5. In the morning, spoon the remaining yogurt into an airtight container.

HOW IT WORKS

The moisture drains from the yogurt, leaving a thick paste that spreads like cream cheese.

EVERY TRICK IN THE BOOK?

Cream of the Crop

- **Make a Substitute for Cream Cheese or Sour Cream in a Dip Recipe.** Blend cottage cheese in a blender until it reaches the consistency of sour cream.
- **Thin Cream Cheese for Use in Dips.** Mix the cream cheese with plain yogurt.
- **Color Cream Cheese for Various Holidays.** Add a few drops of food coloring and mix well.
- **Soften Cream Cheese Without Melting It.** Place the container or block of cream cheese inside a resealable plastic bag and submerge it in warm water for 5 minutes. The warmth of the water softens the cream cheese.

WHEN DO WE EAT?
How to Make Yogurt

WHAT YOU NEED
- 1 quart of half-and-half
- Glass mixing bowl
- Cooking thermometer
- Spoon
- 3 tablespoons of nonfat plain yogurt
- Clean, empty 1-quart glass mayonnaise jar with screw-on lid
- Insulated picnic cooler

WHAT TO DO
1. Pour 1 quart half-and-half into the glass mixing bowl.
2. Using a cooking thermometer, heat the half-and-half in a microwave oven at 50 percent power for 1 min-ute at a time until the temperature

of the half-and-half reaches 180° Fahrenheit. (Use the spoon to stir the liquid between cooking times to prevent scalding and skim off any film from the surface.)
3. Remove from the oven and let cool to 115° Fahrenheit.
4. Add 3 tablespoons of nonfat plain yogurt, mix well, pour into the clean, empty mayonnaise jar, and seal the lid tightly. (Adding the 3 tablespoons of yogurt to the milk when it is above 155° Fahr-enheit may kill the yogurt cultures, which would then prevent the yogurt from forming. Adding more than 3 tablespoons of yogurt to the warm milk will cause overcrowded bacillus, resulting in a sour, watery yogurt.)
5. Place the warm jar inside the insulated picnic cooler, close the lid, and let sit undisturbed for 8 hours. Refrigerate when ready.

HOW IT WORKS
Heating the half-and-half kills any bacteria that might otherwise compete with the yogurt cultures. Yogurt contains living bacteria called *Lactobacillus acidophilus*, which multiply exponentially in warm milk. Three tablespoons of yogurt from this batch can be used to start a new batch, ideally within 5 days.

EVERY TRICK IN THE BOOK

Fun with Yogurt

You can also use yogurt to:

- **Make a Creamy Gelatin Dessert.** Dissolve the flavored gelatin powder in the proper amount of hot water according to the directions on the box and then substitute 1 cup of yogurt for every cup of cold water required.
- **Bake Light, Fluffy Muffins.** Replace the milk called for in a muffin recipe with the same amount of plain yogurt, and add ½ teaspoon of baking soda for each cup of yogurt used.
- **Make Delicious Gravy for Meat or Chicken.** Mix plain yogurt into the pan drippings and add 1 tablespoon of cornstarch for each cup of yogurt to prevent it from separating.
- **Thin Mayonnaise for Use in Recipes.** Add plain yogurt to the mayonnaise and mix well with a whisk.
- **Make a Piecrust Lighter and Flakier.** Substitute plain yogurt for the liquid suggested in the recipe.

How to Make Homemade Cheese with Panty Hose

WHAT YOU NEED

- Clean, used pair of panty hose
- 2 pots
- Water
- Stove
- Tongs
- Large mixing bowl
- 1 galloon of whole milk, pasteurized (not ultra-pasteurized)
- Wooden spoon
- Measuring cups
- ½ cup of white vinegar
- Measuring spoons
- Medium mixing bowl
- 2 teaspoons of kosher salt, ground fine

WHAT TO DO

1. Boil a clean, used pair of panty hose in a pot of water on the stove.
2. Fish out the panty hose with a pair of tongs.
3. Let the panty hose cool to room temperature.
4. Stretch the panty hose over a large mixing bowl.
5. Bring 1 gallon of whole milk to a boil in the second pot on the stove over medium heat, stirring continually with a wooden spoon to prevent scorching.

6. When the milk reaches a boil, turn the heat to low, and add ½ cup of white vinegar, stirring continually.

7. If the solution does not immediately separate into curds (chunks) and whey (yellowish liquid), add more vinegar 1 tablespoon at a time until separation occurs.

8. As soon as the curds and whey separate, pour the solution from the pot through the panty hose and into the mixing bowl, allowing the panty hose to strain out the curds.

9. Remove the panty hose containing the curds from the bowl.

10. Rinse the curds gently through the panty hose with cold water.

11. Squeeze the panty hose over the sink to express all whey from the curds.

12. Empty the curds into a medium mixing bowl.

13. Sprinkle the curds with 2 teaspoons of kosher salt.

14. Place the curds inside the foot of one of the panty hose legs, press the cheese together, and wrap it the panty hose.

15. Let the cheese sit undisturbed at room temperature for 1 to 2 hours.

16. Refrigerate the cheese, which is now ready to use.

HOW IT WORKS

The acetic acid in the vinegar curdles the milk, causing the proteins to coagulate, separating the milk into curds and whey. Boiling water sterilizes the panty hose, and the fine nylon mesh serves as an excellent strainer.

WHEN DO WE EAT?

How to Grate Cheese

Grating cheese yourself costs half as much as purchasing grated cheese, and the flavor of freshly grated cheese far surpasses factory-grated cheeses.

To dry a block of cheese for grating, wrap the block tightly in a sheet of paper towel and set on a counter at room temperature. After the paper towel absorbs sufficient oil from the cheese, discard the paper towel and repeat the process with a fresh sheet of paper towel as many times as you deem desirable.

Before grating the cheese, spray the grater with a thin coat of cooking spray to make cleaning the grater easier. Or use a pastry brush to paint a thin coat of vegetable oil on the grater. Reapply as needed.

To make soft cheeses like Parmesan or Romano easier to grate, place it in the freezer for 15 minutes before grating.

Wear a metal thimble on each finger when grating cheese to avoid injuring your fingertips.

Avoid making a mess when grating cheese by holding the grater inside a large resealable plastic bag and then grate the cheese inside the bag. When you finish, the bag—not the kitchen countertop—will contain the grated cheese.

Or if grating cheese into a bowl, before you start, dust the inside of the bowl with a pinch of flour. Doing so prevents the grated cheese from sticking to the inside of the bowl.

Four ounces of cheese yields 1 cup of grated cheese.

To clean a cheese grater, rub the grater with a raw potato to push the chunks of cheese from the holes.

If you don't have a grater, use a potato peeler or carrot peeler to cut cheese into decorative strips to be added to salads or as garnishing to any meal.

How to Sour Milk with Vinegar

WHAT YOU NEED

- Measuring cups
- 1 cup of milk
- Measuring spoons
- 1 tablespoon of white vinegar (or lemon juice)
- Drinking glass
- Saucer

WHAT TO DO

1. Let the milk sit in its carton at room temperature for 1 hour.
2. Mix 1 cup of milk and 1 table-spoon of white vinegar (or 1 tablespoon of lemon juice) in a drinking glass at room temperature.
3. Cover the drinking glass with the saucer.
4. Let the mixture sit for 5 minutes at room temperature.
5. Use the soured milk in your recipe as directed.

HOW IT WORKS

The acetic acid in the vinegar (or the citric acid in the lemon juice) curdles the milk's casein proteins, causing the milk to separate or "clabber."

MILKING A DUCK

- You can also sour milk by substituting ½ tablespoon of cream of tartar for the vinegar or lemon juice in the above directions. Use a fork to whisk the milk to make sure the cream of tartar is thoroughly dissolved.
- The baking soda in many recipes requires soured milk to trigger its leavening power.
- Sour milk is often called for in recipes as a substitute for buttermilk in baked goods.
- Sour milk is also used as a starter ingredient for yogurt and cheese making.
- Milk that has gone sour on its own is spoiled and is unsafe to use in recipes. Several families of bacteria turn the milk sour and unpalatable by excreting lactic acid.

EVERY TRICK IN THE BOOK

Sour Grapes

You can also use vinegar to:

- **Wash Insecticides from Vegetables.** Fill your kitchen sink with cold water and add 1 cup of white vinegar. Immerse the vegetables in the solution for 10 minutes, and scrub them gently with a clean sponge to loosen any residue. Rinse clean with cold water.
- **Minimize the Odor of Cooking Cabbage.** Fill a drinking glass halfway with white vinegar and set the glass near the stove. Vinegar absorbs odors.
- **Prevent Beans from Giving You Gas.** Soak the beans overnight in a pot of water and add ¼ cup of apple cider vinegar. The next morning, wash the beans, refill the pot with fresh water and 2 tablespoons of apple cider vinegar, and cook as usual.
- **Keep Beets Bright Red.** Add 2 tablespoons of white vinegar to the cooking water and boil the beets in their skins, leaving at least 2 inches of stem.
- **Bake a Moist and Fluffy Chocolate Cake.** Add 1 teaspoon of white vinegar to the baking soda when mixing the batter. The vinegar helps neutralize the sharpness of the baking soda.
- **Prolong the Firmness of Gelatin.** Add 1 teaspoon of white vinegar for every 4 cups of liquid when preparing the powder.
- **Reduce the Amount of Cooking Oil Absorbed by Fried Food.** Add 1 tablespoon of white vinegar to the frying pan before heating the oil.
- **Sweeten a Strong-Tasting Onion.** Slice and separate the onion into rings, mix 1 teaspoon of white vinegar in a bowl of cold water, and soak the onion rings in the solution for 30 minutes.
- **Help Peeled Potatoes Retain Their Firmness and Whiteness.** Add 1 tablespoon of white vinegar to the cooking water.
- **Store Peeled Potatoes for Up to Three Days.** Place the potatoes in a large bowl filled with enough cool water to cover them, add 1 teaspoon of white vinegar, cover the mouth of the bowl with a sheet of plastic wrap, and refrigerate.

How to Separate Egg Whites with a Water Bottle

WHAT YOU NEED

- Eggs
- Shallow bowl
- Second bowl
- Clean, empty water bottle

WHAT TO DO

1. Break the eggs (without breaking the yolks) into the shallow bowl and discard the shells.
2. Holding the clean, empty water bottle upside down at a 45-degree angle, and squeezing it gently to remove some of the air from the bottle, place the mouth of the bottle over one of the yolks.
3. Stop squeezing the bottle to allow the bottle to suck in more air and the yolk.
4. Hold the mouth of the bottle over the second bowl, and squeeze the bottle to drop the yolk into the bowl.
5. Repeat until you move all the egg yolks into the second bowl.

HOW IT WORKS

Squeezing the bottle removes some of the air from the bottle. When you stop squeezing the bottle, it returns to its original shape, creating a vacuum to suck up the yolk.

EGG ON YOUR FACE

- Separating the egg white from the yolk is easier if the eggs are cold.
- A yolk can also be separated from the egg white by cracking the egg open in the clean, cupped palm of your hand and letting the egg white slip through your fingers into a bowl. The yolk will remain in your palm.

- Breaking the egg into a small funnel placed in the top of tall drinking glass allows the egg white to slip through the funnel, leaving the yolk behind.

EVERY TRICK IN THE BOOK

Spin the Bottle

You can also use a water bottle to make:

- **Bird Feeders.** Poke two chopsticks through the bottom half of the bottle to make a perch for the birds, cut additional holes for the birds to reach the birdseed, and fill the bottom of the bottle with birdseed. Cap the bottle, and tie string (or dental floss) around the lip of the bottle to hang it from a tree branch.

- **Boot Trees.** Insert two clean, empty water bottles in a pair of boots to keep them standing tall in the closet.
- **Cupcake Protectors.** Using a pair of scissors, carefully cut off the bottom half of a water bottle and use it to cover a cupcake.
- **Hot caps.** Cut an empty water bottle in half with a pair of scissors, and place the top half of the bottle over seedlings. Take off the cap for ventilation, and replace the cap at night to retain heat and moisture.

How to Poach an Egg with a Pineapple Can

WHAT YOU NEED

- Empty pineapple slices can, 8 ounces
- Dishwashing liquid
- Towel
- Can opener
- Butter
- Skillet
- Boiling water
- Stove
- Egg
- Measuring cup
- Tongs
- 2 plates
- Spatula

WHAT TO DO

1. Wash an empty 8-ounce pineapple can with soapy water, rinse clean, and dry.
2. With a can opener, remove the bottom from the can.
3. Grease the inside of the can thoroughly with butter.
4. Place the prepared can on the floor of the skillet.

5. Pour ½ inch of boiling water into the skillet.
6. Turn on the heat on the stove to simmer the water.
7. Crack an egg into a measuring cup, and then pour the egg into the pineapple can.

8. When the egg is thoroughly cooked, use tongs to carefully remove the hot pineapple can from the skillet and place it on a plate to cool.

9. Use a spatula to carefully remove the egg from the skillet and place it on a second plate.

10. Serve.

11. Wash the can for reuse, or recycle it.

HOW IT WORKS

The pineapple can becomes a poaching ring to contain the uncooked egg, preventing the egg from spreading through the pan of water. The butter prevents the poached eggs from sticking to the ring.

WHEN DO WE EAT?
How to Boil the Perfect Egg

To prevent the eggs from cracking and to make the shells easier to peel, pierce the large end of each eggshell with a clean sewing needle.

Place the eggs in a single layer in a saucepan and cover them with cold water, at least 1 inch above the tops of the shells. Cover the saucepan with a lid and set the stove on medium heat. When the water comes to a full boil, remove the saucepan from the heat.

For large soft-cooked eggs, let the eggs sit in the hot water for up to 4 minutes. For large hard-cooked eggs, let the eggs sit in the hot water for 15 to 17 minutes. Egg whites harden at 176° Fahrenheit. Egg yolks harden at 185° Fahrenheit.

Drain the hot water (leaving the eggs in the saucepan), and immediately cover the eggs with cold water. Doing so prevents a dark greenish ring from forming around the yolk of a hard-boiled egg.

For soft-cooked eggs, let the eggs stand in the water until they are cool enough to handle. For hard-cooked eggs, let the eggs stand in the cold water until they cool completely.

How to Make Fluffy Scrambled Eggs with Cream of Tartar

WHAT YOU NEED

- 2 eggs
- Medium bowl
- Measuring spoons
- ⅛ teaspoon of cream of tartar
- 1 tablespoon of butter
- Small saucepan
- Stove
- Whisk
- 1 dash of salt
- 1 dash of pepper

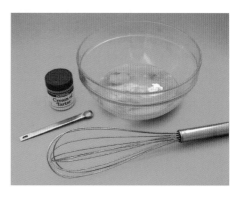

WHAT TO DO

1. Crack the eggs into the bowl and add ⅛ teaspoon of cream of tartar.
2. Put 1 tablespoon of butter in the saucepan and heat it on medium on the stove to coat the inside of the pan.
3. Using the whisk and holding the bowl at a slight angle, beat the eggs for 2 minutes. Aside from mixing the yolks and the whites together,

the whisking action aerates the eggs and allows the cream of tartar to break up the proteins, allowing them to better coagulate.

4. When the butter starts to sizzle, pour the beaten eggs into the pan. Let the eggs cook, undisturbed, until they form a fluffy yellow bottom layer.

5. Using the spatula, move cooked eggs to the middle of the pan, allowing the uncooked eggs to spill into the pan.
6. While the eggs are still runny, add salt and pepper to taste, then flip the eggs to cook them to the desired consistency.

HOW IT WORKS
The acids in cream of tartar stabilize egg whites by lowering the pH of the mixture, creating fluffy scrambled eggs.

ALL YOUR EGGS IN ONE BASKET
- Another way to make fluffy scrambled eggs: mix in 1 teaspoon of baking soda and 1 teaspoon of water for every two eggs when beating the raw eggs.
- To make light scrambled eggs, add a pinch of cornstarch when beating the raw eggs.
- To cook up tender scrambled eggs, grease the top half of a double boiler with butter, and cook the eggs over the hot water, assuring a consistent and uniform low temperature.
- To make creamy scrambled eggs, grease a saucepan with butter, cook the eggs slowly over a low heat on the stove, and at the very end, mix in 1 tablespoon of evaporated milk.

How to Identify Hard-Boiled Eggs with Food Coloring

WHAT YOU NEED

- Eggs
- Saucepan with lid
- Cold water
- Food coloring (red, blue, or green)
- Stove

WHAT TO DO

1. Place the eggs in a single layer in a saucepan and cover them with cold water, at least 1 inch above the tops of the shells.
2. Add 10 to 20 drops of food coloring (red, blue, or green) to the water.
3. Cover the saucepan with a lid and set on the stove on medium heat.
4. When the water comes to a full boil, remove the saucepan from the heat.
5. Let the eggs sit in the hot water for 15 to 17 minutes.
6. Drain the hot water (leaving the eggs in the saucepan), and immediately cover the eggs with cold water.
7. Let the eggs stand in the cold water until they cool completely.
8. Store the hard-boiled eggs alongside raw eggs in the refrigerator.

HOW IT WORKS

The food coloring tints the shells of the hard-boiled eggs, making them easy to identify and distinguish from raw eggs when stored in the refrigerator.

EGGISTENTIAL THOUGHTS

- If you're all out of food coloring, adding 1 tablespoon of Tang orange drink mix, 1 teaspoon of Kool-Aid drink mix, or 1 teaspoon of Jell-O powder to the boiling water also tints the eggshells.

- Another way to color the shells of hard-boiled eggs so you can differentiate them from raw eggs in the refrigerator: mark the hard-boiled eggs with a brightly colored crayon, a pencil, or an indelible marker.

- If you neglected to mark the hard-boiled eggs, spin the eggs on the counter. Hard-boiled eggs spin smoothly. Raw eggs wobble.

EVERY TRICK IN THE BOOK
Color My World

You can also use food coloring to:

- **Make Noodles More Festive.** Add 10 drops of food coloring to the water when cooking noodles to dye them.
- **Cook Up Colorful Mashed Potatoes.** Add a few drops of food coloring to the mashed potatoes (green for St. Patrick's Day, orange for Halloween, and red for Valentine's Day).
- **Color Cream Cheese.** Add a few drops of food coloring and blend.
- **Enrich Potato Salad.** Add a few drops of yellow food coloring to the mixed ingredients and stir well.
- **Make Unbuttered White Rice Appear Buttered.** Add a few drops of yellow food coloring to the water before adding the rice.

How to Give a Soufflé a Tasty Crust with Potato Chips

WHAT YOU NEED
- Bag of potato chips
- Rolling pin
- Soufflé mold
- Vegetable shortening
- Soufflé batter

WHAT TO DO

1. Run over a bag of potato chips with a rolling pin, breaking the chips into fine crumbs.
2. Before filling the soufflé mold with batter, grease the mold well with vegetable shortening.
3. Dust the mold with the potato chip crumbs.
4. Fill the mold with batter, and cook according to the recipe.

HOW IT WORKS
The crushed potato chips give the soufflé a unique yet tasty crust.

LET THE CHIPS FALL WHERE THEY MAY
- Seal open bags of potato chips with a clothespin or clear packaging tape, which adheres and re-adheres.
- Potato chips stay fresh when wrapped and stored in the freezer. Surprisingly, they don't get soggy when they thaw.
- Crushed potato chips can be used as a substitute for bread crumbs in most recipes that call for bread crumbs.

How to Make Whipped Cream with a Jar

WHAT YOU NEED

- Glass jar with lid, 1 quart
- Refrigerator with freezer compartment
- Measuring spoons
- 2 tablespoons of confectioner's sugar
- Measuring cups
- 1 cup of heavy cream
- 1 teaspoon of vanilla extract
- Spoon
- Bowl (optional)

WHAT TO DO

1. Chill the glass jar in the freezer for 15 minutes.
2. Add the confectioner's sugar, heavy cream, and vanilla extract to the jar.
3. Seal the lid tightly.
4. Shake the jar vigorously in all directions for 3 minutes.
5. With a spoon, taste the whipped cream to check its consistency. If not whipped enough, replace the lid, and shake vigorously for another minute.
6. Refrigerate for 10 minutes.
7. Serve the whipped cream from the jar, or spoon it into a bowl.

HOW IT WORKS

The air inside the jar whips and aerates the cream.

CRÈME DE LA CRÈME

- Cream must be below 50° Fahrenheit to whip into foam. At 50° Fahrenheit or above, the cream churns into butter.
- Heavy cream and whipping cream are two different types of cream. Heavy cream contains at least 36 percent fat content. Whipping cream contains between 30 and 36 percent fat content. While both creams can be used to make whipped cream, heavy cream produces a dense whipped cream. Whipping cream produces a fluffy, billowy whipped cream.
- To make whipped cream for use as cake icing, dissolve 1 teaspoon of unflavored powdered gelatin in 2 tablespoons of boiling water. Let cool to room temperature, and then add the solution to the recipe just before shaking the jar. The gelatin stabilizes the whipped cream.

EVERY TRICK IN THE BOOK

A Jarring Experience

You can also use a jar to:

- **Prevent a Steel Wool Pad from Rusting.** Dissolve 3 tablespoons of baking soda in a jar filled halfway with water, and store the steel wool pad in the solution.
- **Beat an Egg.** Break the egg into a clean, empty jar, seal the lid shut, and shake well.
- **Make Cinnamon Sugar.** Place 2 or 3 sticks of cinnamon in a jar, cover with sugar, seal the lid, and let sit undisturbed for a few weeks to allow the cinnamon to infuse the sugar.

6

MEAT AND SEAFOOD

Whenever I make meatballs, I insist they be the same size and shape—not just for aesthetic reasons, but because uniformly sized meatballs finish cooking together at the same time.

To achieve the same size and shape, I grab the ice cream scooper and scoop up the prepared ground beef mixture. I pop the lump of beef into the palm of my hand, roll it into a ball, and place it on a baking sheet.

The first time my wife, Debbie, walked into the kitchen to find me scooping ground beef with an ice cream scoop, she nearly fainted. She truly thought I was filling ice cream cones with beef.

When I explained that the scooper grabs the perfect amount of beef, she held out her open palm. I gave her a scoop of beef, and she began shaping meatballs.

"Handle the meat as little as possible to guarantee tender balls," I told her.

She rolled her eyes. "You've been saving that line just for me, haven't you?"

"No, I've been saving this ice cream scooper just for you."

How to Bulk Up Bacon with Flour

WHAT YOU NEED

- 2 plates
- Knife
- Cutting board
- Flour
- Stove
- Paper towel
- Clean, empty soup can
- Aluminum foil

WHAT TO DO

1. Place the bacon strips on a plate, and let sit to bring the uncooked bacon to room temperature.

2. Using a knife and a cutting board, slice the strips into halves.

3. Pour the flour onto the second plate.

4. Dip both sides of the bacon strips in the flour before frying on the stove.

5. After frying, drain the excess grease from the strips by placing them on a sheet of paper towel (or between two sheets), allowing the paper towel to absorb the fat.

6. Rather than pouring bacon drippings down the drain, which will eventually clog the drain, pour the drippings into a clean, empty soup can, seal with a piece of aluminum foil, and place in the freezer to harden the fat. When the can is full, discard it in the garbage.

HOW IT WORKS

The flour adheres to the fat in the bacon, and when fried, the bacon absorbs the flour, which plumps up the strips and prevents them from shrinking as much as bacon fried without a flour coating.

BRINGING HOME THE BACON

- To prevent bacon from curling in the frying pan, soak the uncooked strips in cold water for a few minutes.
- To make bacon curls, fry the bacon strips until halfway cooked and remove the bacon from the skillet. Twirl each individual strip around the tines of a fork, and pierce with a toothpick to hold the curl together. After preparing all the strips of bacon, broil the assembled curls over a low flame until crisp.

- To store cooked bacon in the freezer, line a cookie sheet with waxed paper, place the bacon strips on the paper, and freeze. Once the bacon strips have frozen, transfer them into a resealable plastic bag.

How to Turn Overcooked Chicken into Chicken Salad with Mayonnaise

WHAT YOU NEED

- Sharp kitchen knife
- 3 cups of cooked chicken
- Large bowl
- Fork
- ¼ cup of mayonnaise
- 3 stalks celery, finely chopped
- 1 cup of raisins
- 2 teaspoons of lemon juice
- ½ teaspoon of salt
- ¼ teaspoon of ground black pepper

WHAT TO DO

1. If your chicken breasts get dried out in the oven, use a sharp kitchen knife to cut the chicken into bite-sized chunks.
2. In a large bowl, use a fork to blend the mayonnaise, celery, raisins, lemon juice, salt, and pepper.
3. Add 3 cups of the chicken chunks to the bowl, and toss to coat with the mixture.
4. Serve.

HOW IT WORKS

Mayonnaise revives the dry chicken chunks, turning it into a tasty treat.

CHICKEN FEED

- To give the above recipe a different flare, prepare as directed but substitute ½ Granny Smith apple, finely chopped, for the celery.
- To give the above recipe an Indian flavor, prepare as directed but substitute 2 cups of seedless grapes for the raisins and add 1 teaspoon of curry powder and 1 teaspoon of honey to the mixture.
- You can also turn overcooked chicken into chicken soup. Simply shred the meat and add it to broth.

How to Cook Bratwurst with a Coffee Can and Beer

WHAT YOU NEED

- 1 six-pack of bratwurst, 16 ounces
- Clean, empty coffee can
- 2 cans of beer
- 1 white onion, chopped
- 2 tablespoons of fresh rosemary, diced
- Barbecue grill or campfire
- Oven mitt
- Tongs
- Knife
- 6 bratwurst buns
- Mustard, ketchup, or other condiments

WHAT TO DO

1. Place the brats in standing upright in the empty coffee can.
2. Pour the beer over the brats.
3. Add the onion and rosemary.
4. Cook over a barbecue or campfire (with a medium-high heat), using a grill to support the coffee can, for 25 minutes or until the brats are firm.
5. Using an oven mitt, carefully remove the coffee can from the barbecue or campfire.
6. Using tongs, remove one brat and cut it open with a knife to make sure the meat is cooked through to the center. If not, cook the brats in the beer for another 5 to 10 minutes and retest. Or parboil the brats in beer for 15 minutes and finish cooking them on the grill.
7. Serve the brats on buns, and dress with the condiments of your choice. Add some onions from the coffee can if desired.

HOW IT WORKS

Boiling bratwurst in beer adds aromatic flavors and moisture to the mild sausages usually made of veal, pork, or beef.

WHEN DO WE EAT?
How to Prevent Cooking Odors

- **Broccoli.** Cooking a stalk of celery with broccoli prevents the broccoli from emitting a strong odor. Or place a slice of stale white bread in the cooking water. After cooking, discard the bread.
- **Brussels Sprouts.** To prevent odors from pervading the house when cooking brussels sprouts, place one or two slices of stale white bread in the cooking water. After cooking, discard the bread.

- **Cabbage.** To minimize the odor of cooking cabbage, fill a drinking glass halfway with white vinegar and set the glass near the stove. Vinegar absorbs odors. Or add a few unshelled walnuts to the cooking water in the pot. To reduce the odor of cooking cabbage and simultaneously enhance the taste, mix 2 tablespoon of lemon juice in the cooking water before adding the cabbage. Or place a slice of stale white bread on top of the cabbage to absorb the odor; when finished cooking, discard the bread.
- **Cauliflower.** To eliminate any pungent odors when cooking cauliflower, place a few unshelled walnuts into the pot of cooking water. Or place a slice of stale white bread on top of the cauliflower as you steam the vegetable. The bread absorbs the odors.
- **Chicken.** To deodorize uncooked chicken or turkey and simultaneously improve the taste, mix 2 tablespoons of lemon juice and ¼ teaspoon of salt, and massage the solution into the skin of the plucked fowl.
- **Doughnuts.** To eliminate the odor of hot fat when frying doughnuts, add 1 tablespoon of vinegar to the fat before heating.
- **Fish.** To neutralize the smell of fresh fish, dissolve 2 tablespoons of baking soda in 4 cups of water, and soak the fish fillets in the solution for 10 minutes. Then rinse the fillets clean under running water. The sodium bicarbonate lowers the pH of the fish. To absorb the odors of cooking fish, fill a bowl with fresh coffee grounds and place the bowl on a countertop near the stove. The coffee grounds absorb the harsh smells.

How to Revive Overcooked Meat with Beef Broth

WHAT YOU NEED

- Meat fork
- Sharp knife
- Cutting board
- Frying pan
- Beef broth
- Mushrooms
- Stove
- Pasta, rice, or quinoa

WHAT TO DO

1. Remove the meat from the pan, and using a meat fork and sharp knife, cut it into slices on a cutting board.
2. Place the slices in a pan.
3. Pour a few cups of beef broth over the meat in the pan.
4. Let the meat soak in the broth for 20 minutes.
5. Cover the slices of meat with mushrooms, and simmer on the stove on low heat for 10 minutes.
6. Serve the beef over pasta, rice, or quinoa.

HOW IT WORKS

Adding liquid rehydrates the beef, the broth and mushrooms add flavor, and the pasta, rice, or quinoa help further disguise the blunder.

THE MEAT OF THE MATTER

You can also turn overcooked meat into:

- **Beef Green Curry.** Slice the overcooked beef into cubes. In a frying pan, add 2 tablespoons of green curry paste, 1 teaspoon minced garlic, and 1 tablespoon vegetable oil, and cook for 1 minute. Add two diced green peppers and 13 ounces of coconut cream, add the cubed beef, and bring to a simmer gently for 5 minutes. Season with salt and garnish with ¼ cup chopped coriander. The fat content masks the dry meat.

- **Beef Stroganoff.** Cut the beef into chunks. Caramelize some onions in butter, toss in some sliced mushrooms, and sprinkle flour over the mixture, cooking over medium heat on the stove until the flour turns brown. Add some beef broth and the chunks of beef, simmer the mixture, and add sour cream to thicken. Serve over egg noodles.

- **Short Ribs.** Soak the overcooked beef in prune juice overnight. In the morning, wrap the beef in aluminum foil. Preheat the oven to 225° Fahrenheit, place the wrapped beef in a pan, and heat for 30 to 40 minutes. The aluminum foil traps the moisture. When finished, carefully unwrap the aluminum foil to avoid steam burns.

- **Tacos.** Chop up the dry meat. Dice a small onion and sauté in some olive oil. Add the chopped beef and a small amount of beef broth. Add cumin, oregano, and paprika to taste.

How to Bread Chicken Croquettes with Potato Chips

WHAT YOU NEED

- Rolling pin
- Bag of potato chips
- 2 bowls
- Whisk
- 2 eggs

- Flour
- Chicken breasts
- Stove
- Vegetable oil

WHAT TO DO

1. Run a rolling pin over a bag of potato chips to make fine crumbs.
2. Empty the potato chip crumbs into a bowl.
3. Using a whisk, beat two eggs in a second bowl.
4. To make the chicken breasts easier to handle, dust your hands with flour.

5. Roll the chicken breasts in the potato chip crumbs.

6. Dip the chicken in the beaten egg, and then dip in potato chip crumbs a second time.

7. On the stove, fry the chicken breasts in vegetable oil until brown.

HOW IT WORKS

The beaten egg works like glue to hold the potato chip crumbs to the chicken fillets.

WHEN DO WE EAT?
How to Get the Best Eggs

- Check the carton for the Julian date (the date the eggs were packed). The Julian date is a three-digit number from 001 (representing January 1) to 365 (December 31). Eggs kept refrigerated at 45° Fahrenheit or lower are safe to be consumed four to five weeks beyond the Julian date.

How to Roast Chicken with Mayonnaise, Bread, and Beer

WHAT YOU NEED

- 1 whole chicken
- Measuring spoons
- 1 teaspoon of baking soda
- Pot
- Boiling water
- Tweezers or a strawberry huller
- Mayonnaise
- White bread
- Broiling pan
- 1 can of beer, 12 fluid ounces
- Oven

WHAT TO DO

1. To remove any remaining feathers from a chicken, add 1 teaspoon of baking soda to a pot of water, bring to a boil, and immerse the chicken briefly. Then pluck out the feathers and pinfeathers with a pair of tweezers or a strawberry huller.
2. To give roasted chicken a crisp brown crust, rub mayonnaise over the skin before cooking.

3. Place a few slices of white bread under the rack in the broiling pan. The bread will absorb fat drippings, reducing smoke and the possibility of the grease catching fire.

4. Sit the chicken on the rack in a broiling pan so the chicken can stand upright, adjusting the drumsticks, if necessary, to balance the bird.

5. Pop open the can of beer and place it upright inside the chicken.

6. Roast the chicken.

7. When finished cooking, discard the beer can and serve the chicken.

HOW IT WORKS

The steam from the beer helps cook the bird from the inside, giving the chicken an exceptional flavor.

SPRING CHICKEN

- Roasting a chicken uncovered yields a crisp skin. Roasting a chicken covered keeps the steam inside the bird, cooking the meat faster while retaining moistness.
- To prevent a chicken from overbrowning in the oven, place a tent made from aluminum foil over the chicken after roasting for roughly two-thirds of the cooking time.
- Use a wooden spoon to remove a roasted chicken from the pan. Insert the wooden handle of the spoon into the chicken's cavity and carefully lift up under the breastbone.

EVERY TRICK IN THE BOOK
Beer Blast

You can also use beer to cook:

- **Beef Stew.** Instead of using water or beef stock, add the contents of a can of beer and a packet of onion soup mix.
- **Poached Eggs.** Poach the eggs in beer rather than water.
- **Pot Roast.** If the recipe calls for adding water to the roast, substitute the same amount of beer to enhance the meat.
- **Shrimp.** Boil shrimp in 12 ounces of beer—seasoned with two crushed cloves of garlic, 2 teaspoons of kosher salt, and 2 teaspoons of freshly ground black pepper—for 4 to 5 minutes.

How to Cook Hamburgers for a Crowd with Aluminum Foil

WHAT YOU NEED

- 10 pounds of ground beef
- 2 plastic lids (the size of 16-ounce cottage cheese container lids)
- Baking pan
- Aluminum foil
- Oven
- Barbecue grill (optional)

WHAT TO DO

1. Place ¼ pound of ground beef on top of a plastic lid.
2. Place the second plastic lid on top of the ground beef and press down gently, spreading the meat to form a circular patty.
3. Trim the excess meat from around the patty.
4. Remove the top lid, and peel the patty from the bottom lid.
5. Line the bottom of a baking pan with sheet of aluminum foil, and cover with neat rows of single hamburger patties.
6. Cover the patties with a second sheet of aluminum foil, and arrange the second tier of hamburgers on the aluminum foil.

7. Repeat step 2 to create a third and fourth tier of patties.

8. Bake in an oven set at 350° Fahrenheit for roughly 35 minutes. Or bake for 20 minutes and finish cooking each patty on an outdoor barbecue grill.

HOW IT WORKS

Using the plastic lids helps form perfect patties, and the aluminum foil reflects and evenly distributes the heat in the oven, cooking all the hamburger patties equally, producing juicy and tender hamburgers.

WHERE'S THE BEEF?

- To cook up moist hamburgers, add one stiffly beaten egg white or one grated medium onion to each pound of ground beef.

- Cook up a crusty hamburger by dipping the ground beef patty in flour before frying.

- Before stacking raw hamburger patties on a platter, cover the platter with a sheet of plastic wrap to avoid contaminating the plate with raw meat. After moving all the patties to the grill, remove the plastic wrap from the platter, discard the tainted plastic wrap, and place the finished hamburgers on the clean platter.

- Before freezing uncooked hamburger patties, punch a hole roughly the diameter of a nickel through the center of each patty. The hole allows you to cook the frozen hamburger patties without thawing them first. As the burger cooks, the center will not remain raw and the hole will close back up.

How to Stretch Meatloaf with Rolled Oats

WHAT YOU NEED

- Bowl
- Whisk
- 1 egg
- 1½ pounds of ground beef
- ¾ cup of uncooked rolled oats
- ¾ cup of onion, finely chopped
- ½ cup of ketchup
- 1 tablespoon of Worcestershire sauce
- 2 cloves of garlic, minced
- ½ teaspoon of salt
- ½ teaspoon of black pepper
- Resealable freezer bag, gallon size
- Baking pan, 10 inches x 6 inches

- Cooking spray
- Oven
- Meat thermometer
- Knife
- Spatula

WHAT TO DO

1. In the bowl, use the whisk to lightly beat the egg.
2. Place the ground beef, oats, chopped onion, ketchup, beaten egg, Worcestershire sauce, garlic, salt, and black pepper in the gallon-size resealable freezer bag. Seal the bag closed, and squeeze the bag to blend lightly but thoroughly.
3. Spray the inside of the pan with cooking spray.
4. Shape the meatloaf mixture into a loaf, open the bag, and slide the loaf into the pan.
5. Preheat the oven to 350° Fahrenheit.
6. Bake the meatloaf for 50 to 55 minutes or until the temperature of the meatloaf is 160° Fahrenheit.

7. Remove from the oven, and let sit for 5 minutes before slicing with a knife and serving with a spatula.

HOW IT WORKS

The oats absorb and retain the juices from the meat, creating a moist and delicious meatloaf that yields six to eight servings.

BEEF IT UP

- Blending the contents (or half the contents) of a packet of onion soup mix into the meatloaf mix spices up the finished loaf.
- Mixing some tomato juice into the meatloaf mix before baking helps create a tender and juicy loaf.
- Misting some cold water over the top of the meatloaf before placing the pan in the oven prevents the meatloaf from cracking in the oven.
- To cut the baking time in half, place individual servings of meatloaf in a muffin tin rather than one large loaf in its own pan.
- To frost a meatloaf with lightly browned mashed potatoes, prepare 1 cup of mashed potatoes or instant potatoes. Approximately 15 minutes before the meatloaf finishes cooking, spread the mashed potatoes over the meatloaf like icing on a cake, and continue baking it in the oven.

EVERY TRICK IN THE BOOK
Sow Your Oats

You can also use rolled oats to:

- **Thicken Soup.** To give soup a rich consistency, add 1 or 2 tablespoons of rolled oats.
- **Bind Veggie Burgers.** After making a base for black bean burgers, add a handful of rolled oats to help hold the burgers together and retain moisture.
- **Create Whole Grain Flour.** Using a blender, grind rolled oats into powder. Mix 2 cups of powdered oats with 1 cup of all-purpose flour to create dough for breads, cookies, and cakes.
- **Make Oat Milk.** In a blender, puree 1 cup of rolled oats with 3 cups of water until smooth.
- **Boost a Smoothie.** When making a smoothie, add 1 or 2 tablespoons of rolled oats to add bulk.
- **Thicken Stew.** Add 1 or 2 tablespoons of rolled oats to the stew, and simmer for 5 to 10 minutes until thick.

How to Marinate and Tenderize Meat with Coca-Cola

WHAT YOU NEED

- Sharp knife
- Meat fork
- 2½ to 3 pounds of brisket
- Large frying pan
- Stove
- Slow cooker
- 1 can of Coca-Cola, 12 fluid ounces
- 1 bottle of chili sauce, 12 ounces
- 1 packet of onion soup mix
- Cutting board
- 1 onion
- 20 baby carrots
- Carving fork
- Carving knife

WHAT TO DO

1. Using a sharp knife and meat fork, cut the brisket in half.
2. Brown the two halves of brisket in the large frying pan on the stove over medium heat.
3. Place the two browned brisket halves in the slow cooker.
4. Empty the can of Coca-Cola, bottle of chili sauce, and packet of onion soup mix into the slow cooker.

5. Using a sharp knife and a cutting board, chop the onion and place the slices on top of the brisket in the slow cooker.
6. Add the baby carrots to the slow cooker.
7. Simmer for 2½ hours or until the meat is tender.
8. Use a carving fork to move the brisket to a cutting board. Let sit for 10 minutes.
9. With a carving knife, slice and serve.

HOW IT WORKS

The acids in the Coca-Cola tenderize and flavor the meat, making it melt in your mouth.

EVERY TRICK IN THE BOOK
The Real Thing

You can also use Coca-Cola to:

- **Bake an Excellent Barbecue Sauce.** Mix equal parts Coca-Cola and ketchup. For thicker sauce, add more ketchup. To spice up the sauce, add a few drops of Tabasco Pepper Sauce or ¼ cup of Worcestershire sauce.
- **Stop Beans from Causing Flatulence.** Add half a can of Coca-Cola to the water while cooking the beans.
- **Bake Delicious, Moist Brownies.** Substitute Coca-Cola for the water called for in the recipe.
- **Cook Cranberries.** Add ¼ teaspoon of Coca-Cola, reducing the need for sugar.
- **Bake a Moist Ham.** Wrap the ham in aluminum foil in a pan, and baste with 1 can of Coca-Cola. For the last half hour of cooking, remove the aluminum foil and allow the ham to bake directly in the cola. The cola and juices from the ham make delicious gravy.
- **Tenderize Beef or Pork.** Place the meat in a resealable plastic bag, pour 1 can of Coca-Cola into the bag, and marinate in the refrigerator for 2 or 3 hours.
- **Roast a Turkey.** Wash the uncooked bird, place it in a plastic oven bag, and pour half a can of Coca-Cola over the turkey. Seal the bag and roast. Before the last half hour, split the bag open to allow the turkey to bake to a nice caramel brown. The Coca-Cola provides the salt, so there's no need to add any.

WHEN DO WE EAT?
Amazing Marinades

Sitting for several hours or days in an acidic marinade flavors and tenderizes meats, poultry, and fish. Marinate the item in a reseal-able plastic bag, eliminating the need to stir marinade in bowl. Instead, you simply turn over the bag. Squeeze out as much air as possible to maximize the marinade's contact with the surface of the meat or fish. Here are some simple yet tasty marinades:

- **Lemon Juice.** Place the fish or meat in ¼ cup of lemon juice per pound, and let sit for 20 to 30 minutes before cooking.
- **Milk.** Marinate chicken breasts in milk for 3 hours in the refrigerator before baking.
- **Olive Oil and Vinegar.** Mix equal parts olive oil and white vinegar, rub the mixture into both sides of the meat, and let sit for 2 hours in the refrigerator.
- **Papaya Juice.** Marinate meat in papaya juice in the refrigerator for 3 to 4 hours. Papain, an enzyme in papaya, tenderizes meat.
- **Vinegar.** Place fish in a resealable plastic freezer bag, add ¼ cup of white vinegar, and let sit for 20 to 30 minutes before cooking. The vinegar destroys bacteria and sweetens the fish. For meat, use ½ cup of vinegar on a 4- to 6-pound roast, add whatever herbs you desire, and let sit overnight on a shelf in the refrigerator. Prepare the meat without draining or rinsing the vinegar.

How to Truss a Turkey or Chicken with Dental Floss

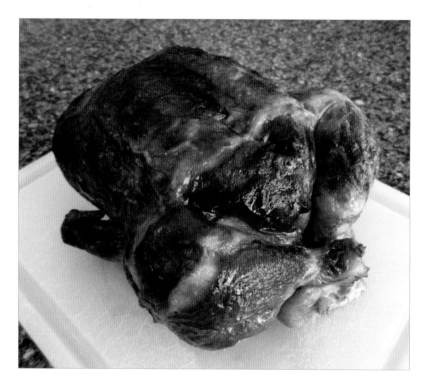

WHAT YOU NEED

- Thawed turkey or chicken
- Dental floss
- Scissors

WHAT TO DO

1. Tuck the wingtips behind the drummets of the thawed bird.
2. With the legs facing away from you, slide the middle of a long piece of dental floss under the tail of the bird, and, as if tying shoelaces, tie a knot to hold the two drumstick ends against the tail.
3. Make a second knot to hold the drumsticks in place.
4. Pull the ends of the dental floss around and under the thighs.
5. Flip the turkey or chicken on its back, and tuck each end of dental floss under each wing.
6. As if tying shoelaces, tie the two ends together around the waist of the turkey or chicken, and tie a knot with a bow.

7. Using a pair of scissors, trim the excess dental floss.

8. Flip the bird over, season, and roast.

HOW IT WORKS

Dental floss is strong and durable enough to truss poultry.

TALKING TURKEY

- Trussing a turkey or chicken—keeping the drumsticks and wings close to the body—ensures even cooking by maintaining the bird's shape in the oven.
- Trussing isn't required to cook a turkey or chicken, but the finished bird comes out more evenly roasted and looking more tightly packed and professional.
- Before trussing a turkey or chicken, make sure the bird is thawed to room temperature, and remove the neck and organs from the cavity.

EVERY TRICK IN THE BOOK
Loose Strings

You can also use dental floss to:

- **Slice Cheese Neatly.** Wrap a long piece of dental floss around your opposing forefingers as if you were going to floss your teeth and press it through the block of cheese.

- **Cut Cookie Dough.** Slide a strand of dental floss under the roll of dough, cross the two ends over the top of the roll, and pull.
- **Prepare a Jar of Preserves for Easy Opening.** Before sealing a jelly jar with melted paraffin wax, place a strand of dental floss across the mouth of the jar, letting it rest on the surface of the jelly inside the jar with the ends hanging over the rim. Pour the paraffin over the strand of dental floss. When you're ready to open the jar, pull up the string to lift the layer of paraffin.

How to Poach a Fish with Panty Hose

WHAT YOU NEED

- Scissors
- Clean, used pair of panty hose
- Water
- Paper towels
- Wide, short pan with lid
- Poaching liquid
- Measuring spoons
- Lemon juice
- Waxed paper
- Toothpick (or fork)
- Stove
- Reusable rubber kitchen gloves
- Serving platter

WHAT TO DO

1. With a pair of scissors, cut off one leg from a clean, used pair of panty hose.
2. Trim the panty hose leg to the size of the fish.
3. Rinse the fish thoroughly with water, and pat dry with paper towels.
4. Place the fish inside the panty hose leg.
5. Place the fish, clad in the panty hose leg, in a wide, short pan.
6. Add enough poaching liquid to cover the fish.
7. For every pound of fish, add 2 tablespoons of lemon juice to the poaching solution before cooking. The lemon juice helps the fish maintain its original density, producing a firmer and whiter cooked fish (except in the case of salmon, which will be pinker).

8. Cover the pan with a sheet of waxed paper. Using a toothpick (or the tines of a fork), poke a small hole in the center of the waxed paper.

9. Secure the pan's lid in place over the waxed paper.

10. Bring the poaching liquid to a simmer on the stove over medium heat.

11. Cook the fish for 10 minutes or until the center of the fish appears opaque and flakes easily when prodded with a fork.

12. To remove a fish from poaching liquid, put on a pair of reusable plastic kitchen gloves and use your gloved hands to lift the fish, wrapped in the panty hose, from the pan to a serving platter.

13. Use a pair of kitchen scissors to carefully cut off the panty hose.

14. Serve.

HOW IT WORKS

The nylon hose holds the fish together, preventing it from falling apart during poaching.

A FINE KETTLE OF FISH

- Poaching, a fancy term for cooking fish or any food in a gently simmering liquid, is healthier than frying.
- Poaching leaves fish moist, succulent, and tender.
- The simplest poaching liquid is water, but you can also use vinegar, broth, dry white wine, or milk. For flavor, add some lemon juice, garlic, onions, celery, carrots, herbs, and spices.

EVERY TRICK IN THE BOOK
Something Fishy

Several household products neutralize fish odor:

- **Baking Soda.** To deodorize a pungent fish before cooking it, dissolve 2 tablespoons of baking soda in 1 quart of water, soak the fish fillets in the solution for 10 minutes, and rinse the fillets under running water.
- **Coffee.** To absorb the harsh odors of cooking fish, fill a bowl with fresh coffee grounds and place the bowl on a countertop near the stove.

How to Defrost Frozen Fish with Milk

WHAT YOU NEED

- Hot water
- Paper towels
- Baking pan (or glass baking dish)
- Milk (whole or 2 percent)
- Plastic wrap
- Refrigerator

WHAT TO DO

1. Rinse the frozen fish fillets under hot running water to melt most of the ice.
2. Pat the fish fillets dry with a sheet of paper towel.
3. Place the frozen fish in the pan (or glass baking dish), and cover the fish with milk.
4. Cover the pan with plastic wrap.
5. Place the covered pan in the refrigerator overnight (or a minimum of 8 hours), allowing the fish to defrost in the milk.
6. Remove the pan from the refrigerator, and remove the fish from the milk.
7. Blot the fish with a sheet of paper towel. Do not rinse the milk off the fish.
8. Proceed cooking the fish with whatever recipe you wish to follow.

HOW IT WORKS

The fat in the milk eliminates the frozen taste and absorbs the fishy flavors. The lactic acid in the milk tenderizes the fish, giving the fish an astoundingly fresh taste.

CHILL OUT

- Never defrost frozen fish at room temperature on the kitchen counter. Doing so allows bacteria to proliferate quickly, increasing the chances of food poisoning. Instead, thaw frozen fish in the refrigerator.
- To keep fish fresh for up to two days, rinse the fish under cold water and pat dry with paper towels. Place the entire fish or fillets in a colander or large strainer set over a bowl. Place ice cubes on top of the fish up to the rim of the strainer, and put the bowl in the refrigerator. Or place the fish on a cake rack in a pan, fill the pan with crushed ice, and refrigerate. The ice cools the fish to 32° Fahrenheit, prevents the fish from deteriorating, and melts into the bowl or pan, washing bacteria from the fish.

- To keep fish for more than two days, rinse the fish under cold water and pat dry with paper towels, then wrap it tightly in plastic wrap, followed by aluminum foil, and freeze for up to two weeks.

How to Clean Clams with Cornmeal

WHAT YOU NEED

- Measuring cup
- Salt
- Cold, fresh water
- Large pot or bowl
- Measuring spoons
- Cornmeal
- Resealable plastic bag
- Freezer (optional)
- Boiling water (optional)
- Beer-can opener (or knife)

WHAT TO DO

1. To encourage wild clams to expel sand, for every 1 dozen clams, dissolve ⅓ cup of salt in 1 gallon of water in a large pot or bowl. To prevent disease or food poisoning, make sure the water remains continuously colder than 50° Fahrenheit.

2. For every 1 dozen clams, add 1 tablespoon of cornmeal to the water, and mix well.

3. Place the clams in the solution and let sit undisturbed for 12 hours. Change the salt water, and repeat two more times for a total of 48

hours. (Clams use up the oxygen in the water roughly every 12 hours, clamp up, and stop purging debris.)

4. To the pry clams from their shells, wash them in cold water, place them a resealable plastic bag, and either freeze for 30 minutes or immerse in boiling water for 3 minutes.

5. Open the clams with a beer-can opener or knife.

HOW IT WORKS

The clams open their shells, stick out their siphons, feed on the cornmeal, and expel grit and sand. Placing the clams in boiling water or a freezer relaxes their muscles, making them easier to open.

CLAM UP

- Never soak saltwater clams in fresh water. They clam up and, unable to breath the oxygen in the fresh water, die.
- After steaming clams, pour the liquid from the pot into a reusable plastic container, let cool to room temperature, and freeze. Substitute the flavorful liquid for water the next time you cook rice to create a tastier dish.
- Failing to purge the grit from clams tends to leave sand in the bottom of your bowl of clam chowder.
- Swishing soft-shell clams in broth before dipping them in melted butter rinses away the sand.
- Clams make their shells primarily from calcium carbonate found in the ocean.

EVERY TRICK IN THE BOOK
Enjoy Your Meal

You can also use cornmeal to:

- **Prevent Corn Bread from Sticking to the Baking Pan.** Before adding the corn bread batter to the pan, grease the inside of the pan with vegetable shortening and then dust with cornmeal.
- **Give Fried Chicken a Chewy Coating.** Instead of coating the uncooked chicken parts with bread crumbs or flour, use cornmeal.
- **Make Cornmeal Pancakes.** Add ¼ cup of cornmeal for every 1 cup of all-purpose flour used in the recipe.

WHEN DO WE EAT?
Cooking with a Clothes Dryer

Author Carolyn Wyman, who pioneered food product reviewing pre-Internet as the junk-food-loving co-author of the "Supermarket Sampler" syndicated newspaper column, published this recipe for shrimp cooked in a clothes dryer. Carolyn's books include *Better than Homemade* and *The Great American Chocolate Chip Cookie Book*.

CLOTHES DRYER SHRIMP

What You Need
- 1½ teaspoons of Old Bay or other favorite seasoning (optional)
- ½ pound of extra-large unpeeled shrimp
- Aluminum foil
- 1 laundry hosiery bag

What to Do
1. Sprinkle the Old Bay or other seasoning over the unpeeled shrimp, if desired, and toss to distribute evenly.
2. Wrap the shrimp in aluminum foil. You can put up to four in a foil packet, but put them side by side rather than on top of one another.
3. Seal tightly, then double or even triple wrap with aluminum foil. (Good wrapping is essential to avoid fishy dryer syndrome.)
4. Place the foil package in the laundry hosiery bag, close, and toss in the dryer alone. Run the dryer at the high setting for 10 to 12 minutes. Peel and eat. Serves two.
5. Note: Because dryer temperatures vary, you might want to check the package for doneness at 8 minutes. You can also cook shrimp while clothes are being dried, but it will take quite a bit longer.

Reprinted from The Kitchen Sink Cookbook: Offbeat Recipes from Unusual Ingredients *by Carolyn Wyman (Birch Lane Press/ Carol Publishing). Visit Carolyn at www.carolynwyman.com*

7

PASTA, SAUCES, AND SOUPS

In the 1960 movie *The Apartment*, bachelor C. C. Baxter (Jack Lemmon) uses a tennis racket as a colander to strain a pot of cooked spaghetti.

Of course, some of the noodles slip through the interlaced strings, but a tennis racket works much better than lifting spaghetti from the pot of hot water with tongs, pouring the steaming water from the pot by holding the lid slightly askew with a dishtowel, or draining the pasta through a bandana, a plastic beach bucket strainer, or a detached window screen.

So I decided to improve upon the tennis racket.

To make the latticed strings less porous, I inserted the head of the tennis racket into a clean pair of panty hose. When I swung the tennis racket, the nylon legs swished back and forth in the breeze. I demonstrated my invention for my wife, Debbie.

"Tennis, anyone?" I said.

"Prozac, anyone?" she replied.

How to Fix Lumpy Gravy or Sauce with a Strainer

WHAT YOU NEED

- Metal strainer
- Mixing bowl
- Tablespoon

WHAT TO DO

1. To remove lumps from your sauce, let the gravy or sauce cool for a few minutes.
2. Place a metal strainer over a mixing bowl.
3. Pour the gravy or sauce into the strainer.
4. Use a tablespoon to push the gravy through the strainer.

HOW IT WORKS

Gravies and sauces get lumpy if the flour used is not sifted. Pushing the gravy through a metal strainer sifts the lumps of flour, producing a smooth and creamy gravy or sauce.

THE REST IS GRAVY

- If you don't have a strainer, pour the lumpy gravy into a blender, make sure the lid is secured tightly, and puree.
- Sifting the flour before adding it to the gravy prevents lumps. Sifting aerates the flour. To sift flour properly, simply pour the flour into a strainer and gently tap the side (or stir with a wooden spoon) to sprinkle aerated flour or dust a countertop.
- Another key to avoiding lumpy gravy: add the flour slowly and whisk frequently.
- Yet another tip to prevent lumps: mix the flour with enough hot water to make a paste, and then stir the paste into the juices.

WHEN DO WE EAT?
Last-Minute Substitutes

- **Baking chocolate, unsweetened (2 ounces):** Use ⅓ cup of unsweetened powdered cocoa and 1 tablespoon of melted butter.
- **Baking powder (1 teaspoon):** Mix ½ teaspoon of cream of tartar and ¼ teaspoon of baking soda.

- **Buttermilk (1 cup):** Use 1 cup of plain nonfat yogurt. Or add 1 tablespoon of lemon juice or vinegar to a cup, fill the rest of the cup with milk, and let sit for 5 minutes.
- **Corn Syrup, Light (1 cup):** Use 1 cup of sugar and ¼ cup of water.
- **Cornstarch (1 tablespoon):** Substitute 2 tablespoons of flour.
- **Eggs (1 egg):** If baking a cake, use 1 teaspoon of baking soda and 1 teaspoon of white vinegar. If cooking anything other than cake, use 1 teaspoon of cornstarch.
- **Milk (1 cup):** Use ½ cup of evaporated milk and ½ cup of water. Or use 3 tablespoons of powdered milk mixed in 1 cup of water.
- **Mustard, Dry (1 teaspoon):** Use 1 tablespoon of prepared mustard.
- **Self-Rising Flour (1 cup):** In a measuring cup, mix 1½ teaspoons of baking powder, ½ teaspoon of salt, and fill the rest of the cup with all-purpose flour.
- **Sour Cream (1 cup):** Use 1 cup of plain yogurt. If cooking the yogurt, add 1 tablespoon of cornstarch to each cup of yogurt to prevent it from separating. To make an excellent sour cream substitute, stir 2 teaspoons of white vinegar into 1 cup of cream at room temperature, and let the mixture sit for 30 minutes.
- **Sugar (1 cup):** Substitute ¾ cup of pancake syrup. In a pinch, substitute 1 cup of molasses for every ¾ cup of granulated sugar. (To compensate for the molasses, decrease the amount of liquid called for in the recipe by 5 tablespoons for every cup of molasses used, and add 1 teaspoon of baking soda to the dry ingredients for every cup of molasses used.)
- **Vegetable Shortening (1 cup):** Use 1 cup and 3 tablespoons of butter.

How to Rescue Burned Gravy with Peanut Butter

WHAT YOU NEED

- Spoon
- Peanut butter, creamy
- Stove

WHAT TO DO

1. Remove the saucepan containing the burned gravy from the stove.
2. With a spoon, carefully remove any burned particles from the gravy in the saucepan.
3. Add 1 tablespoon of creamy peanut butter for each cup of gravy, and stir over a low heat on the stove.

HOW IT WORKS

The peanut butter masks the burned taste, and you won't detect the taste of the peanut butter.

RIDING THE GRAVY TRAIN

- The peanut butter method also works to fix burned tomato sauce.
- All out of peanut butter? Pour the burned gravy into a clean pan, add sugar (½ teaspoon at a time, tasting as you go), and stir.

EVERY TRICK IN THE BOOK
From the Peanut Gallery

You can also use peanut butter to:

- **Make "Ants on a Log."** Fill celery stalks with creamy peanut butter and sprinkle with raisins.
- **Tame the Odor of Frying Fish.** Add 1 teaspoon of creamy peanut butter to the pan while frying fish to mellow the stench and add a pleasant taste.
- **Sweeten Hot Chocolate.** Add 1 tablespoon of creamy peanut butter to the hot chocolate, and stir well to dissolve it.

How to Thicken Thin Sauce with Cornstarch

WHAT YOU NEED

- Measuring spoons
- Cornstarch (for cornstarch-based sauce) or flour (for flour-based sauce)
- Water (for cornstarch-based sauce)
- Bowl
- Wooden spoon
- Saucepan

- Stove
- Butter (for flour-based sauce)

WHAT TO DO

For Cornstarch-Thickened Sauce:

1. For every cup of sauce that needs thickening, mix 1 teaspoon of cornstarch and 1 tablespoon of water in a bowl.
2. Pour the mixture into the warm sauce, stirring quickly with the wooden spoon.
3. Bring the sauce to a boil in a saucepan (which cooks the cornstarch), and then let the sauce simmer for 1 minute to give the sauce sufficient time to permeate the cornstarch with flavor.

For Flour-Thickened Sauce:

1. For every cup of sauce that needs thickening, knead 2 teaspoons of butter into 2 teaspoons of flour in a bowl.
2. Add the dough to the warm sauce, stirring quickly with the wooden spoon.
3. Bring the sauce to a boil in a saucepan(which cooks the flour), and then let the sauce simmer for 2 minutes to give the sauce sufficient time to flavor the flour.

HOW IT WORKS

When sauce made with cornstarch is boiled too long, the cornstarch loses its ability to thicken. Adding more cornstarch thickens the sauce.

A roux made with flour loses its ability to gel as it browns in the pan. Adding a blend of flour and fat (in this case, butter) allows the additional flour to mix with the excess water in the sauce, creating a smooth sauce.

HIT THE SAUCE

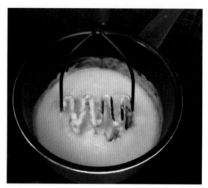

- When cooking white sauce, stir with a potato masher, which can be used to remove lumps.
- When making egg-based sauce, use moderate heat. Boiling an egg-based sauce causes it to curdle.
- If a sauce begins to separate on the stove, add 1 teaspoon of cold water.

EVERY TRICK IN THE BOOK
Through Thick and Thin

You can also use cornstarch to:

- **Make Fluffy Omelets.** When beating the raw eggs, add a pinch of cornstarch to the mixture.
- **Prevent Pastry Dough from Sticking to the Cutting Board and Rolling Pin.** Before rolling out the dough, sprinkle cornstarch on the cutting board and rolling pin to absorb excess moisture. The cornstarch does not alter the flavor of the dough.
- **Enhance Hot Chocolate.** Stir a pinch of salt and 1 teaspoon of cornstarch into the hot chocolate to make it thick and smooth.

- **Make Incredibly Smooth Icing.** Add 1 teaspoon of cornstarch to the icing mixture.
- **Inhibit Custard Made of Egg Yolks, Milk, and Sugar from Curdling.** Beat 1 teaspoon of cornstarch into the cold milk for every 4 egg yolks used.
- **Make Tasty Cake Sauce.** Save the liquids drained from canned fruits, thicken to the consistency of cream with cornstarch, and warm in a saucepan on the stove over low heat.
- **Prevent Hard Candy from Sticking Together.** Place the hard candies in a serving bowl and, before serving, sift a dash of cornstarch over them.

WHEN DO WE EAT?
The Best Ways to Thicken Gravy

For starters, pour the pan of meat or poultry drippings into a tall drinking glass, and let it sit undisturbed for 10 minutes. The grease will rise to the surface. Spoon it out and discard it.

Pour the glass of drippings into a saucepan.

To make clear gravy, mix cornstarch with enough water to make a smooth paste in a bowl. For opaque gravy, mix all-purpose flour and enough water (or beef bouillon for a richer flavor) to make a smooth paste in a bowl. Add either mixture gradually to the drippings in the saucepan, stirring the gravy continuously while bringing it to a boil.

To thicken clear gravy and keep it translucent, add powdered arrowroot or potato starch.

To darken pale gravy, dissolve 1 tablespoon of sugar in 1 tablespoon of water, heat the mixture on the stove in a heavy saucepan until the sugar starts to caramelize, and then mix the pale gravy into the sugared pan.

Enrich the taste of meat gravy by adding 1 or 2 tablespoons of tomato paste. Simmer gently for 20 minutes, stirring frequently.

If you notice any pools of fat floating on the surface of the finished gravy, use a slice of white bread to sop it up.

How to Save Mushy Pasta with Olive Oil

WHAT YOU NEED

- Colander
- Medium saucepan
- Measuring spoons
- 2 teaspoons of olive oil
- Stove
- Serving dish
- Parmesan cheese, grated
- Parsley sprigs

WHAT TO DO

1. If you leave a pot of boiling pasta on the stove too long, drain the pasta through a colander.

2. In a medium saucepan, warm 2 teaspoons of olive oil over medium heat on the stove.

3. Add the pasta to the saucepan, and sauté for 3 to 7 minutes.

4. Transfer the pasta to a serving dish.

5. Top with Parmesan cheese and parsley sprigs.

HOW IT WORKS

Sautéing crisps the pasta, and the Parmesan cheese masks the overcooked flavor of the noodles, allowing you to salvage dinner.

WHEN DO WE EAT?
How to Cook Pasta to Perfection

Fill a large pot with 3 quarts of water for every ½ pound of pasta you intend to cook, giving the pasta plenty of room to grow. When cooked, raw pasta absorbs water, doubling in volume.

Before turning on the heat, dissolve 1 teaspoon of salt and 1 tablespoon of olive oil for every 3 quarts of water in the pot. The salt helps bring the water to a boil more rapidly and gives the pasta a faint salty taste. The olive oil prevents the pasta from boiling over and helps stop the cooked pasta from sticking together or to the sides of the pot.

Bring the salted water to a rolling boil. Do not add the pasta before the water starts boiling. Doing so slows the water from boiling, causing the pasta to stick together.

Instead, once the water is boiling, stir in the pasta gradually (to avoid lowering the water temperature), cover the pot, turn off the heat, and let sit undisturbed for 20 minutes. Do not lift the lid during those 20 minutes and let the valuable steam escape.

Pour the pasta into a colander, run under hot water, and drain.

Wait for the pasta to stop steaming before serving. (If you place steaming pasta on a plate, the steam condenses, creating a puddle of water on the plate.)

How to Fix Broken or Curdled Hollandaise Sauce with an Egg

WHAT YOU NEED

- Whisk
- 1 egg yolk
- Small saucepan
- Stove

WHAT TO DO

1. If the hollandaise sauce breaks, place the sauce aside.

2. Whisk 1 egg yolk in the saucepan over low heat on the stove until the yolk turns thick and pale.
3. Slowly add the broken hollandaise sauce to the yolk, whisking vigorously.

HOW IT WORKS

The egg yolk unifies the hollandaise sauce, making it slightly thicker than usual but with the expected taste.

AWESOME SAUCE

- Hollandaise sauce "breaks" when the clarified butter separates from the egg yolks or excessive heat causes the yolks to scramble and turn into clumps.
- To prevent hollandaise sauce from separating when warmed for a long time, beat 1 teaspoon of cornstarch into the egg when making the sauce.
- The traditional recipe for hollandaise sauce uses undercooked eggs, which can cause salmonella.
- To fix curdled hollandaise sauce, remove the sauce from the heat, and whisk in 1 teaspoon of hot water without reheating the sauce.

- Another way to fix curdled hollandaise sauce: place the hollandaise sauce in a saucepan, and whisk in 1 teaspoon of sour cream at a time until the sauce is smooth.

How to Make Salad Dressing with Mayonnaise and Yogurt

WHAT YOU NEED

- Bowl
- Whisk
- Measuring cups
- 1 cup of plain yogurt
- ½ cup of mayonnaise
- Measuring spoons
- 1 teaspoon of mustard
- 1 tablespoon of lemon juice
- ¼ teaspoon of paprika
- ½ teaspoon of garlic powder

WHAT TO DO

1. In a bowl, whisk together the yogurt, mayonnaise, mustard, lemon juice, paprika, and garlic powder.
2. Refrigerate or use immediately.
3. Use as salad dressing or dip for fresh vegetables.

HOW IT WORKS

Yogurt transforms mayonnaise into creamy, rich salad dressing, and various spices make it even more flavorful.

How to Make Cheese Sauce with Skim Milk

WHAT YOU NEED

- Sharp knife
- Leftover cheeses
- Cutting board
- Medium saucepan
- Skim milk
- Stove
- Spoon

WHAT TO DO

1. To make a tasty cheese sauce from leftover cheeses, use a sharp knife to cut up chunks of leftover cheese on a cutting board.

2. Place the chunks of cheese in a medium saucepan.

3. Add a small amount of skim milk.

4. Warm over a low heat on the stove, and stir continuously to prevent the cheese from separating or becoming stringy.

5. Use the cheese sauce to top noodles or vegetables.

HOW IT WORKS

Melting the cheese blends it all together, and adding skim milk makes the sauce creamy.

Hot to Make Fresh Tomato Sauce with a Grater

WHAT YOU NEED

- Kitchen knife
- Cutting board
- 2 fresh, ripe tomatoes, large
- Box grater
- Large bowl
- Olive oil
- Salt
- Pepper
- Basil, fresh

WHAT TO DO

1. Using a kitchen knife and a cutting board, slice two fresh, ripe tomatoes in half.

2. Stand the box grater inside the large bowl, hold it in place, and carefully and gently rub the cut side of one of the tomato halves against the coarse side of the box grater, allowing the grater to peel the pulp from the tomato skin.

3. Repeat with the remaining tomato halves.

4. Remove the box grater from the bowl.

5. Add olive oil, salt, and pepper, and mix well.

6. Heat up the homemade tomato sauce, pour over cooked pasta, and add fresh basil.

HOW IT WORKS

Rubbing a ripe tomato against a grater removes the pulp from the tomato—without blanching, peeling, or chopping.

TOMAYTO, TOMAHTO

- Be careful when grating tomatoes to avoid cutting yourself on the grater. Keep your fingers flat and parallel to the surface of the grater, or better yet, wear gloves.
- When using a grater, you can protect your fingertips from accidents by wearing a metal sewing thimble on each finger.
- One pound of tomatoes yields approximately 1½ cups of tomato pulp.
- To make the tomato sauce thinner, pour the grated tomato pulp into a blender and puree for 1 minute.
- Adding 1 teaspoon of sugar to tomato sauce can help balance the acidity and enhance the sweetness of the tomatoes.

EVERY TRICK IN THE BOOK

Grate Ideas

You can also use a grater to:

- **Chop Onions or Garlic.** Instead of chopping or mincing, you can grate onions or garlic.
- **Create Fresh Bread Crumbs.** Grate a piece of dry toast.
- **Make Citrus Zest.** Instead of cutting and mincing lemon or orange peel, grate it.
- **Melt Chocolate Faster.** Grated chocolate melts faster than chopped chocolate.
- **Recycle Soap.** Save and grate slivers of soap. In a pot, melt the grated soap, pour into a mold (like a clean, used tuna fish can), let cool, and pop out a new bar of soap.
- **Shred Vegetables.** Grate potatoes for latkes, hard-boiled eggs and carrots for salads, or zucchini for bread.

How to Spice Up Spaghetti Sauce with Coffee

WHAT YOU NEED

- Measuring spoons
- 1 teaspoon of instant coffee grounds
- 1 teaspoon of hot water
- Coffee cup
- Jar of store-bought spaghetti sauce
- Saucepan
- Stove
- Wooden spoon

WHAT TO DO

1. To flavor store-bought spaghetti sauce, dissolve 1 teaspoon of instant coffee grounds with 1 teaspoon of hot water in a coffee cup.
2. While heating the spaghetti sauce in a saucepan on the stove on low heat, pour the coffee solution into the spaghetti sauce.
3. Stir well with a wooden spoon while heating.

HOW IT WORKS

Coffee enriches spaghetti sauce, adding a deep roasted flavor that takes the edge off the sweetness of the tomatoes.

NOODLING AROUND

- Once you open a jar of spaghetti sauce, keep it stored in the refrigerator and use within 5 to 10 days.
- Store-bought spaghetti sauce does not typically contain any preservatives. If the sauce in an opened jar darkens from bright red to maroon, the sauce has gone bad.

EVERY TRICK IN THE BOOK

Coffee Break

You can also use coffee to:

- **Clean a Griddle.** Let the griddle cool to the touch, pour a pot of hot coffee on the surface, and wipe dry with a clean cloth. Many short-order cooks use this tip nightly to clean the grill.
- **Absorb the Stench of Spoiled Food from Your Freezer.** Empty the freezer, fill a bowl with fresh coffee grounds, place the bowl in the freezer, and shut the door. Let sit undisturbed for several days.
- **Flavor Roasted Lamb.** Baste the lamb with 1 cup of hot coffee for a sensational taste.
- **Deodorize a Refrigerator.** Place a bowl filled with fresh coffee grounds on the back shelf.
- **Degrease Cooked Sausage.** Mix 1 or 2 tablespoons of instant coffee with enough hot water to make a paste. Moments before the sausage finishes cooking, add the coffee to the pan. The coffee absorbs the grease and flavors the sausage.
- **Make Red-Eye Gravy.** Fry ham, add water to the drippings, and add 1 teaspoon of instant coffee.
- **Give Bottled Barbecue Sauce a Cajun Twist.** Dissolve 1 tablespoon of instant coffee in 1 tablespoon of water, and add it to the barbecue sauce, blending well.

- **Neutralize the Stench of Cooking Fish.** Fill a bowl with fresh coffee grounds, and place the bowl on a countertop near the stove to absorb the stink.
- **Remove the Smell of Fish, Onions, or Garlic from Your Hands.** Fill your cupped palm with coffee grounds (fresh or used), add a little water if using fresh grounds, rub your hands together for 1 minute, and rinse clean.

How to Strain Fat from Soup with Lettuce

WHAT YOU NEED
- Head of iceberg lettuce
- Tongs

WHAT TO DO
1. To remove fat from a pot of cooked soup, peel off one or two large leaves from a head of iceberg lettuce.
2. Float the dry lettuce leaves on the surface of the soup.
3. Wait a few minutes.
4. When the leaves are coated with fat, carefully fish them out with a pair of tongs and discard.

HOW IT WORKS
The fat in soup clings to leafy vegetables like lettuce.

FAT CHANCE

- The scum floating on the surface of a pot of cooked chicken soup is coagulated protein bound together by fat. When heated, protein coagulates. The fat melts into oil, rises to the surface, and coats the coagulated protein.
- If you refrigerate soup, the fat rises to the surface.
- To strain fat from broth, stretch the waistband of a clean, used pair of panty hose across the mouth of a strainer, colander, pot, or tall bowl. Carefully pour the broth through the hose.
- You can also use ice cubes to skim fat from soup. Using scissors, cut off the foot from a clean, used pair of panty hose, place a few ice cubes inside the foot, and tie a knot in the open end. Or wrap the ice cubes in a sheet of paper towel. Using either method, skim the sachet  over the surface of the soup. The ice attracts the fat, which clings to the nylon hose or paper towel.
- The best kitchen utensil for skimming fat from soups is a skimmer—a tool with a round, flat end covered with a fine-mesh screen.

WHEN DO WE EAT?

How to Thicken Soups

- **Clear Soups.** To thicken soup but keep it clear, add ½ tablespoon of powdered arrowroot for every 1 cup of soup to achieve the consistency of medium cream. Or add ½ tablespoon of cornstarch or potato starch for every 1 cup of soup. To prevent cornstarch from forming lumps in the soup, mix it with  broth or wine to create a thin paste before adding it to the soup.
- **Opaque Soups.** Add 1 tablespoon of flour for every 1 cup of soup. Note that flour turns clear soup opaque. Or add instant mashed potatoes or rolled oats to thicken the soup and give it a rich consistency.

8

BREADS AND DESSERTS

When it comes to putting icing on a cake with a spatula, I might as well be applying stucco to a spare tire with a garden trowel. Instead of creating beautiful swirls and crests, I wind up making lopsided blobs and globs—until it dawned on me to dump the spatula and try using a straight-edge putty knife instead.

Off I went to the hardware store to buy a set of three plastic putty knives, each with a different width blade: 2 inches, 4 inches, and 6 inches.

Now I just place the cake on a turntable, apply a thick coat of icing, and then, holding the blade of the 6-inch putty knife upright against the side of the cake, slowly spin the turntable. The straight edge shaves off the excess icing, giving the icing a smooth finish.

The putty knives also come in handy to cut dough and clean residual dough from the cutting board or countertop. But I guess that's just icing on the cake.

How to Save a Crumbling Cake with Icing

WHAT YOU NEED

- 3 cups of confectioner's sugar
- ⅓ cup of butter, softened
- Medium bowl
- Spoon
- 1½ teaspoons of vanilla extract
- 1 to 2 tablespoons of milk
- Resealable plastic bag
- Scissors
- Spatula
- Assistant (optional)

WHAT TO DO

1. If you neglected to grease the cake pan and the cake came out in chunks, mix 3 cups of confectioner's sugar and ⅓ cup of softened butter in a medium bowl with a spoon.

2. Stir in 1½ teaspoons of vanilla extract and 1 tablespoon of milk.

3. Beat the mixture until it becomes thick and smooth enough to spread, adding more milk, if necessary, a few drops at a time. If the milk thins the icing too much, add more confectioner's sugar, a pinch at a time.

4. Fill a resealable plastic bag with the icing.

5. Twist the bag to force the icing to one bottom corner, seal, and use scissors to snip a small bit off the corner.

6. Squeeze out the icing to "glue" the cake pieces back together—with help from an assistant if necessary.

7. After you reassemble the cake, use the spatula to frost the entire cake.

HOW IT WORKS

The icing works like glue to hold the pieces of cake together, and a thick coat of icing over the entire cake hides all the cracks and imperfections.

ICING ON THE CAKE

- To make homemade icing smoother, add 1 teaspoon of cornstarch to the mixture and blend well.
- To prevent icing made from confectioner's sugar from solidifying and cracking, mix in a pinch of baking powder (not baking soda) or a few drops of lemon juice.
- Adding a pinch of salt to the icing when mixing prevents the icing from granulating.

EVERY TRICK IN THE BOOK
Whip It! Whip It Good!

You can also use whipped cream to:

- **Lighten Coffee.** A dollop of whipped cream floating in a cup of coffee adds an elegant touch and delicious taste.
- **Bake Tender, Juicy Meatloaf.** Mix a dollop of whipped cream into every 1 pound of ground beef before placing the meatloaf mixture in the pan for baking.
- **Whip Up Creamy White Mashed Potatoes.** Spray some whipped cream in a saucepan, heat to just before the cream boils, pour the hot cream into the mashed potatoes, and beat well.
- **Enhance Tomato Soup.** Top each bowl of tomato soup with a dollop of whipped cream and dust it with a pinch of paprika.

WHEN DO WE EAT?
How to Ice a Cake

Before icing a cake, chill the cake in the refrigerator. Icing adheres better to a cold cake.

Cut triangles from a sheet of waxed paper and arrange them, overlapping slightly, to form a circle on a cake plate. Remove the cake from the refrigerator and set it on top of the waxed-paper arrangement.

Dust the naked cake with a light coat of confectioner's sugar to prevent the icing from soaking into the cake.

Apply a thin base coat of icing, and let set for 30 minutes. Apply a second, thicker layer.

To give the icing a glossy finish, aim a blow-dryer on the lowest warm setting about 12 inches away from the cake until the icing starts to melt and the bumps vanish. Then let the icing cool.

Before adding decorative touches to the iced cake, use a toothpick to trace your message or designs on the icing.

To decorate or write your message, fill a clean, empty mustard squeeze bottle with icing and pump it on the cake. Or fill a resealable plastic bag with icing, twist the bag to force the icing to one bottom corner, use scissors to snip a small bit off the corner, and pipe the icing through the hole.

After icing the cake, gently pull the triangles of waxed paper from under the cake, revealing a clean cake plate.

How to Remove a Cake Stuck in a Pan with Plastic Wrap

WHAT YOU NEED

- Plastic wrap
- Freezer
- Butter knife
- Two forks
- Cutting board

WHAT TO DO

1. Let the cake sit in the pan undisturbed until it comes to room temperature.
2. Cover the entire cake with plastic wrap.
3. Place the wrapped cake in the freezer for 6 hours or more.
4. Remove the cake from the freezer.
5. Gently run a butter knife around the sides of the pan.
6. Insert two forks at opposite sides of the cake in the space between the pan and the cake, and gently use the forks like tongs to pry the cake upward.
7. Use the two forks around the entire cake until you have nudged all sides upward.
8. Turn the pan upside down, and tap one edge at a 45-degree angle on a cutting board.
9. Let the cake defrost to room temperature.

HOW IT WORKS

Slowly bringing the cake to room temperature and then freezing it allows the cake to better separate from the metal pan without crumbling.

THAT TAKES THE CAKE

- To prevent a cake from sticking to the pan in the first place, upon removing the cake from the oven, place the pan on top of a dampened dish towel and let sit undisturbed for several minutes. The dampness cools the pan and the cake, allowing the cake to naturally separate from the metal sides.
- Another way to remove a cake stuck to the bottom of the pan: reheat the pan in a warm oven for a few minutes.

EVERY TRICK IN THE BOOK

That's a Wrap

You can also use plastic wrap to:

- **Store Bread in the Freezer.** Wrap the bread tightly in plastic wrap to prevent moisture from escaping, causing freezer burn.
- **Freeze Cranberries.** Spread the cranberries on a cookie sheet, cover with a sheet of plastic wrap, and place in the freezer for 20 minutes. Transfer the frozen berries to a resealable plastic bag, remove as much air as possible from the bag, seal securely, and freeze. Frozen cranberries stay fresh for several months.
- **Make a Moist, Tender Cake.** Wrap the freshly baked cake tightly in plastic wrap and let sit at room temperature for 24 hours before serving. The plastic wrap seals in the moistness.
- **Avoid Cleaning Sticky Ingredients from a Measuring Cup.** Line the inside of the empty measuring cup with a piece of plastic wrap. After pouring honey, molasses, chocolate syrup, or corn syrup from the cup, discard the sticky sheet of plastic wrap.

- **Avoid Staining the Inside of a Plastic Container with Tomato Sauce.** Line the container with a sheet of plastic wrap before adding the red food item.
- **Cut Butter Smoothly into Clean Pats.** Cover the knife blade with plastic wrap before cutting the butter.

How to Repurpose Broken Cakes or Cookies as a Parfait with Whipped Cream

WHAT YOU NEED
- Cake or cookie pieces
- Whipped cream
- Fresh fruit (raspberries, black berries, blue berries, strawberries)
- Large glass bowl or individual parfait glasses

WHAT TO DO
1. If your cakes or cookies break apart, stack the pieces between alternating layers of whipped cream and fresh fruit in a large glass bowl or individual parfait glasses.
2. Chill in the refrigerator until ready to serve.

HOW IT WORKS
The whipped cream and fresh fruit in decorative parfait glasses makes the crumbled cake or cookies look intentional.

THE WAY THE COOKIE CRUMBLES
- To bake moist, tender cookies that don't crumble, substitute buttermilk for the milk in the recipe and add a pinch of baking soda to the cookie batter.
- To keep soft cookies fresh and moist, wrap each cookie in an individual sheet of waxed paper before storing. Or place a slice of white bread in the cookie jar.
- Cookie crumbs can be used as toppings for coffee cake or to make piecrust.
- Adding 2 tablespoons of mayonnaise to cake batter keeps the cake moist and less likely to crumble.
- To keep a finished cake moist and fresh, place the cake and half an apple inside the same airtight container.

WHEN DO WE EAT?
How to Make Croutons

WHAT YOU NEED

- Oven
- Butter knife
- Butter
- White bread, several slices (ideally stale)
- Garlic powder
- Ground thyme
- Sharp knife
- Cookie sheet
- Oven mitt
- Airtight container (or resealable plastic bag)

WHAT TO DO

1. Preheat the oven to 375° Fahrenheit.
2. Using a butter knife, butter both sides of several slices of white bread.
3. Season all the buttered sides with garlic powder and ground thyme.
4. Using a sharp knife, slice the bread into small cubes.
5. Spread the cubes on a cookie sheet, and toast the bread cubes in the oven for 5 minutes.
6. Wearing an oven mitt, carefully remove the cookie sheet, toss the croutons to flip them over, and toast for another 5 minutes or until lightly browned.
7. Let cool.
8. Store the croutons in an airtight container or resealable plastic bag.

How to Make Light and Fluffy Pancakes with Club Soda

WHAT YOU NEED

- Whisk
- Mixing bowl
- 2 cups of biscuit mix (or boxed pancake mix)
- 1 egg
- ½ cup of vegetable oil
- ⅓ cup of club soda
- Griddle or waffle iron

WHAT TO DO

1. Using a whisk, mix all the ingredients in a mixing bowl until well blended. (If using boxed pancake mix, substitute the amount of liquid called for by the recipe with the same amount of club soda.)
2. Pour the batter in 4-inch-diameter circles onto a hot griddle to make pancakes or into your waffle iron to make waffles.
3. Use all the batter, and freeze any leftover pancakes or waffles. The batter cannot be stored for later use. When the club soda loses its carbonation, the batter goes flat.

HOW IT WORKS

The carbonation in the club soda causes the pancakes to rise higher, provided you use the batter before the club soda goes flat.

BATTER UP

- Another way to make fluffy pancakes: Substitute buttermilk for the liquid called for in the recipe, and add a pinch of baking soda to the batter. The acids in the buttermilk trigger the baking soda to emit carbon dioxide, causing the pancakes to puff up.
- To pour batter into round pancakes on a griddle, fill a clean, empty ketchup squeeze bottle with the prepared batter.
- If you sprinkle salt on the griddle before pouring the pancake batter, the pancakes won't stick to the surface.
- To make dessert pancakes, add 3 to 4 tablespoons of confectioner's sugar to the batter or substitute orange juice for the liquid in the recipe.

EVERY TRICK IN THE BOOK
Welcome to the Club

You can also use club soda to:

- **Make Inexpensive Soft Drinks.** Mix one part fruit juice to three parts club soda in a tall drinking glass.
- **Pry Clams or Oysters from Their Shells with Ease.** Soak the clams or oysters in club soda for a few minutes to loosen the muscles and shell hinges.
- **Relieve an Upset Stomach.** Drinking club soda soothes indigestion.
- **Make Fluffy Matzah Balls.** Substitute club soda for the liquid used in the recipe.

How to Bake Bread in a Coffee Can

WHAT YOU NEED

- Can opener
- A clean, empty metal coffee can, 11 ounces
- Vegetable shortening
- Flour
- Cake pan or cookie sheet
- Cutting board
- 2 large mixing bowls
- Measuring cups
- Measuring spoons
- 1 package active dry yeast, ¼ ounce
- Cooking thermometer
- 2¼ cups of warm water, 110°F to 115°F
- 3 tablespoons of sugar
- 1 tablespoon of salt
- 2 tablespoons of canola oil
- 7 cups of all-purpose flour
- Eggbeater or electric hand mixer
- Clean, dry hand towel
- Oven
- Oven mitt
- Knife
- Wire rack

WHAT TO DO

1. Using the can opener, carefully remove the bottom of the clean, empty metal coffee can.
2. Grease the inside of the can thoroughly with a generous amount of vegetable shortening. The shortening will make the bread easy to remove from the can after baking.

3. Dust the inside of the greased can with flour.
4. Stand the can upright on a cake pan or cookie sheet.
5. Coat the working surface of a cutting board or clean countertop with a thin layer of flour for use later.
6. In a large mixing bowl, dissolve the package of yeast in the warm water.
7. Add the sugar, salt, canola oil, and 3 cups of flour to the prepared water.

8. Beat the mixture with an eggbeater or electric hand mixer.
9. Add the remaining flour, ½ cup at a time, until the mixture forms a soft, sticky dough.

10. Turn the dough onto the floured cutting board or countertop and kneed the sticky dough for up to 10 minutes or until it becomes stretchable and doughy.
11. Grease the inside of the second mixing bowl.
12. Place the dough inside the greased bowl and cover with a clean, dry hand towel.
13. Place the covered bowl in a warm place (inside a cool oven with the oven light turned on or on top of a refrigerator or running clothes dryer) until the dough rises and doubles in mass, approximately 1½ hours.
14. Punch the dough down to its original size.
15. Press the dough into the greased coffee can, filling the can halfway full.
16. Cover the open end of the can with a clean, dry hand towel.
17. Let the dough rise until it reaches or rises above the top of the can, approximately 30 to 45 minutes.
18. Bake the dough in the can on the cake pan or cookie sheet in the oven at 375° Fahrenheit for 30 to 35 minutes or until golden brown.
19. Wearing an oven mitt, carefully remove the finished bread from the oven.
20. Use a knife to slice off the protruding ends of the bread.
21. Shake the can gently to remove the cylindrical loaf.
22. Let the loaf cool on a wire rack. Do not let the freshly baked bread cool in the can, otherwise the sides will get soggy.

HOW IT WORKS

The clean, empty coffee can doubles as a pan and mold for making an 11-ounce loaf of bread.

THE GREATEST THING SINCE SLICED BREAD

- To bake bread with a soft crust, use a pastry brush to lightly coat the top of the loaf with vegetable oil or warm butter several times during the baking process.

How to Make Dough Rise with a Heating Pad

WHAT YOU NEED
- Dough
- Oversized pan or bowl
- Plastic wrap
- Heating pad
- Towel

WHAT TO DO
1. To coax dough to rise in a cool room, place the dough in an oversized pan or bowl.
2. Cover the pan or bowl with a sheet of plastic wrap.
3. Place the pan or bowl of dough on a heating pad set on low.
4. Place the towel over the pan and heating pad, forming a tent to contain the heat produced by the heating pad.

HOW IT WORKS
The low, uniform warmth from the heating pad encourages the yeast to metabolize quicker, making the dough rise in half the usual time. The yeast breaks down the sugars in the dough to alcohol and carbon dioxide gas. The alcohol evaporates. The gluten in the dough traps the carbon dioxide gas, causing the dough to rise.

RISE AND SHINE
- Yeast is sensitive to temperature. At less than 50° Fahrenheit, the yeast remains inactive. The yeast metabolizes slowly between 60° and 70° Fahrenheit. The optimum temperature for fermentation is between 90° and 100° Fahrenheit. Above that, the yeast action slows, and temperatures above 134° Fahrenheit kill the yeast.
- Another way to make dough rise: place the pan of dough (covered with a clean dish towel) on top of the refrigerator or on top of a running clothes dryer.
- You can also make dough rise by placing a pan filled with boiling water on the lower rack in the oven, placing the pan of dough on the top rack, and shutting the oven door.

EVERY TRICK IN THE BOOK
The Heat Is On

You can also use a heating pad to:

- **Make Yogurt.** Place the covered bowl (containing the warmed milk and starter) on top of a heating pad set on low to stimulate the bacteria to reproduce faster.
- **Warm Food.** Wrap the heating pad with a towel, place the wrapped heating pad on the dining room table, and place a covered plate of food on top of it to keep the food warm.
- **Warm Cold Feet.** If a space heater is verboten in your office, place a heating pad on the floor under your desk to relieve cold feet, of if your feet get really cold, drape the heating pad over them.

WHEN DO WE EAT?
How to Make Bread Crumbs

You can transform several products, readily available in your kitchen pantry, into excellent substitutes for bread crumbs, all of which can be seasoned with a few shakes of oregano.

- **Cornflakes.** Run cornflakes through the blender, or fill a resealable plastic bag with the cereal and grind it up into crumbs by running over it with a rolling pin.

- **Potato Chips.** Run over an open bag of potato chips with a rolling pin, breaking the chips into whatever size crumbs you wish.
- **Saltine Crackers.** Crush saltine crackers into crumbs, and substitute ¾ cup of cracker crumbs for every cup of bread crumbs needed.
- **White Bread.** Slice off the crust from day-old white bread, toast the bread lightly, gently crumble the bread, and press the crumbs through a metal strainer.

How to Slice Cake with Dental Floss

WHAT YOU NEED
- Dental floss
- Cake spatula

WHAT TO DO

1. Cut a strand of dental floss a few inches longer than the diameter of the cake.
2. Hold the ends of the strand in each hand, making the floss taut.
3. Press the string down to cut the cake in half.
4. Slide the floss out from under the bottom of the cake.
5. Repeat the process, cutting the cake into clean slices.
6. Serve the slices with a cake spatula.

HOW IT WORKS

The dental floss cuts the cake into neat, clean slices. Upscale restaurants embrace this technique to serve cheesecake.

PIECE OF CAKE

- To cut a cake with a knife, use a long knife with a serrated edge.
- Rinse the knife in very hot water to help prevent the knife from sticking, cracking the frosting, or tearing the cake.
- Do not press down into the cake with the knife. Instead, use a gentle sawing motion.
- After every cut, dip the blade of the knife in tall glass of hot water to remove any crumbs or icing, and wipe the knife dry with a towel.

How to Grease a Cake Pan with Flour

WHAT YOU NEED
- Resealable plastic bag
- Vegetable shortening
- Measuring spoons
- 1 tablespoon of flour

WHAT TO DO
1. Wear a resealable plastic bag as a glove to grease the inside of the cake pan with vegetable shortening.
2. When you're finished greasing the pan, turn the bag inside out—to avoid getting any leftover shortening on yourself—and discard the bag.
3. After greasing the pan, sprinkle 1 tablespoon of flour into the pan.
4. Tilt the pan at different angles to give the sides and bottom a light coat of flour.
5. Empty any excess flour into the sink by tapping the sides of the pan.
6. Pour the cake batter into the pan and bake.

HOW IT WORKS
Using solid vegetable shortening to grease a cake pan works better than vegetable oil, which tends to burn, particularly on exposed surfaces. The vegetable shortening also holds the dusted flour to the sides of the pan. The combination of grease and flour dust allows the cake to rise more evenly and makes removing the finished cake much easier.

FLASH IN THE PAN
- As an alternative to greasing and flouring the inside of a cake pan using the above method, mix 5 ounces of vegetable shortening, 1 ounce of vegetable oil, and 1 ounce of flour in a bowl until creamy. Grease the inside of cake pans with the mixture.
- Never grease the pan for angel food and sponge cakes. The batter for these cakes is too delicate to rise to their height without clinging to the sides of the pan. When cooling in an inverted pan, these cakes will fall out of a greased pan, turning them flat and soggy.

• Instead of greasing a cake pan, place the pan on a sheet of waxed paper, trace around the bottom of the pan, cut out the waxed-paper circle, and place it on the floor of the pan. After baking the cake in the pan and letting it cool, gently run a but-

ter knife around the sides of the pan to separate the cake. Invert the cake onto a cooling rack, pull off the pan, and peel off the waxed paper from the top of the cake.

EVERY TRICK IN THE BOOK
Flour Power

You can also use flour to:

- **Remove the Last Bits of Melted Chocolate from a Pan.** Mix in a little flour, and add the floured remains into the cake batter.
- **Prevent Grated Cheese from Sticking to the Inside of a Bowl.** Before you start grating the cheese, dust the inside of the bowl with flour.
- **Make Chicken Croquettes Easier to Handle.** Before dipping the chicken breasts into the egg and bread crumbs, dust your hands with flour.
- **Roast a Moist Chicken.** Mix a thick paste of flour and water, and coat the uncooked chicken with the mixture. As the chicken roasts in the oven, the paste will dry and harden, sealing the moisture inside the bird. Approximately 20 minutes before the chicken finishes roasting, remove the flour coating with a fork to let the skin brown.
- **Prevent Custard from Curdling.** In a custard batter made from egg yolks, milk, and sugar, mix 1 teaspoon of flour into the cold milk for every 4 egg yolks used.
- **Cook Up a Crusty Hamburger.** Dip the entire ground beef patty in flour before frying it in a pan greased with vegetable oil.

How to Prevent the Top of a Cake from Browning with a Pan of Water

WHAT YOU NEED

- Baking pan
- Warm water
- Oven

WHAT TO DO

1. To prevent the top of a cake from browning rapidly when baking, fill a pan with warm water.
2. Place the pan of warm water on the lower rack of the oven.
3. Bake the cake on the upper rack.

HOW IT WORKS

The pan of hot water generates steam, which keeps the cake moist.

LET THEM EAT CAKE

- Before placing the batter in a cake pan, make certain the cake pan is deep enough for the cake. A shallow pan is more likely to cause browning than a deep pan.
- Lining the sides of the cake pan with two layers of brown paper and two layers of baking paper rising 2 to 3 inches above the rim of the pan helps protect the top of the cake from browning.
- To prevent the top of a cake from browning, halfway through baking place a sheet of aluminum foil loosely over the top of the cake pan.

How to Stop Nuts and Raisins from Sinking in a Cake with Flour

WHAT YOU NEED

- Nuts or dried fruit
- Baking sheet
- Waxed paper
- Oven
- Resealable plastic bag
- All-purpose flour
- Cake batter
- Mixing spoon

WHAT TO DO

1. Before adding the nuts, raisins, or cranberries to cake batter, place the nuts or dried fruit on a baking sheet lined with waxed paper and heat them in the oven at 325° Fahrenheit for 3 minutes (or until warm).

2. Place the nuts, raisins, and cranberries in a resealable plastic bag, add a little all-purpose flour, and shake well until the nuts and dried fruit are evenly coated with flour.

3. Add the powdered ingredients to the nearly finished cake batter, and stir well until the nuts, raisins, or cranberries are distributed equally.

HOW IT WORKS

Nuts and dried fruits tend to wear a light film of vegetable oil that makes them sink to the bottom of the batter as the cake rises during baking. The thin coat of flour helps the nuts, raisins, and cranberries grip the cake batter and rise with the cake.

THAT SINKING FEELING

- Another simple way to prevent nuts, fruit, and raisins from sinking to the bottom of a cake: warm them in the oven and roll them in butter before mixing them in the cake batter.

- Dusting chocolate chips or chopped dates with flour and then folding them into cake batter prevents them from sinking to the bottom of the cake.
- Coating blueberries with flour keeps them spread throughout muffin batter.

WHEN DO WE EAT?
How to Make Brown Sugar

Using a fork, mix ¼ cup of dark molasses (unsulfured mild) with 1 cup of granulated sugar in a bowl. Add more molasses to darken the sugar, if desired.

Molasses is the thick syrup that results when sugar is extracted from sugarcane or sugar beets. To refine sugar, manufacturers extract juice from sugarcane or sugar beets, boil it down to a syrupy mixture, and then remove the sugar crystals. During the process, the juice is boiled three times. The first boiling produces light molasses (used for baking and as a pancake syrup). The second boiling yields dark molasses (used to flavor baked beans), and the third boiling brings forth blackstrap molasses (put into service to boost fertilizer or livestock feed).

Sulfured molasses results when sulfur dioxide is used in the extraction process.

How to Rescue Burned Piecrust with Whipped Cream

WHAT YOU NEED

- Grater, fine holed
- Knife
- Whipped cream
- Confectioner's sugar
- Spatula (optional)
- Premade pie dough (optional)
- Oven (optional)

WHAT TO DO

1. If you burn a thin layer along the top of a piecrust, use a fine-holed grater to gently scrape away the burned spots.
2. If the edges of the piecrust are burned, use a knife to cut them off.
3. Pump some whipped cream around the edge between the pie and the pan to create ornamentation.
4. Sprinkle some confectioner's sugar on the piecrust to mask the taste of any burns.
5. If the crust is burned beyond repair, use the knife to cut off the top crust and remove it with a spatula.
6. Replace the top with a premade pie dough, and bake in the oven for an additional 12 to 15 minutes.

HOW IT WORKS

Pumping whipped cream around the edges of the pie covers up the fact that you've cut away the burned crust.

A PIECE OF THE PIE

- To prevent a pie from burning, bake the pie on the bottom rack in the lower third of the oven so the heat cooks the pie upward from the bottom up rather than downward from the top.
- Before baking, use a gravy brush to give the top crust a light coat of cold water. The water keeps the top moist and yields a light, flaky crust.
- When the piecrust turns golden brown in the oven, cover it with a sheet of aluminum foil, folding the edges around the pie crust, allowing the inside of the pie to bake without burning the crust.
- Bake the pie on a cookie sheet lined with aluminum foil to catch any overflow.

How to Cover Up a Cracked Cheesecake with Sour Cream

WHAT YOU NEED

- Measuring cups
- 3 cups of sour cream
- ⅔ cup of sugar
- Measuring spoons
- 1 teaspoon of vanilla extract
- Mixing bowl
- Whisk
- Spatula

WHAT TO DO

1. To cover up the cracked surface of a cheesecake, combine 3 cups of sour cream, ⅔ cup of sugar, and 1 teaspoon of vanilla extract in a mixing bowl with a whisk.
2. Using a spatula, spread the mixture over the top of the cheesecake.
3. Bake the cheesecake at 250° Fahrenheit for roughly 15 minutes.
4. Let cool to room temperature before chilling.

HOW IT WORKS

The sour cream glaze fills in and covers the cracks, turning golden brown.

SWEET AND SOUR

- Another way to conceal a cracked cheesecake: cover the top with freshly cut strawberries.
- Cheesecakes crack due to overbaking or an oven set too hot. Either remove the cheesecake from the oven 10 minutes before the recipe suggests, or set the oven to a lower temperature and bake it for a longer time. To check for doneness, remove the cheesecake from the oven when a 3-inch diameter in the center still looks moist, and shake the pan. If the cheesecake is finished baking, the center should jiggle slightly. When it cools, the center will solidify.

How to Create a Cream-Filled Cupcake with a Soda Can

WHAT YOU NEED

- Scissors
- 1 clean, empty aluminum soda can
- Masking tape
- Resealable plastic bag
- Vanilla icing
- Spatula

WHAT TO DO

1. Let the cupcake cool to room temperature.
2. Using a pair of scissors, carefully cut off the top and bottom of the aluminum soda can.
3. Cut a single vertical line through the can, creating one long sheet of aluminum, being careful not to cut yourself on the sharp aluminum.

4. Cut the aluminum sheet into long rectangles, approximately 2 inches wide.
5. Starting from a corner of one of the rectangles, roll the rectangle into the shape of a cone.
6. Secure the cone together tightly with masking tape.

7. Trim the large opening of the cone to remove any sharp points.
8. Snip off one of the bottom corners of the resealable plastic bag, making a small hole to accommodate the aluminum cone.
9. Holding the aluminum cone inside the plastic bag, slide the slender tip of the cone through the hole, pushing it to stretch the plastic firmly and tightly around it.

10. From outside the bag, tape the plastic bag to the aluminum cone to hold it securely in place.

11. Fill the resealable plastic bag with vanilla icing, and seal the bag almost completely shut, leaving a small opening for air to escape. Make sure the icing is firm enough to hold its

shape, but not so stiff that it doesn't pipe easily. Unfortunately, you can learn the proper consistency only through trial and error.

12. Insert the narrow end of the aluminum cone into the center of the top of the cupcake to create a hole about 1 inch deep in the middle of the cupcake.

13. Slowly pipe 1 to 2 tablespoons of icing through the cone into the center of the cupcake until you just barely feel the cupcake swell.

14. Remove the cone from the cupcake.

15. Using a spatula, cover the top of the cupcake with icing to hide the hole.

HOW IT WORKS

The alumni cone doubles as a nozzle, and the plastic bag doubles as a pastry bag.

JUST DESSERTS

- You can make a star-tipped nozzle by using the scissors to snip a jagged edge along the tip of the aluminum cone. Increasing the size of the opening creates beads of icing of various thicknesses.

- When piping icing through the nozzle, exert mild pressure to prevent the bag from popping or the nozzle from shooting off the corner of the bag.

- You can also add filling to cupcakes by hollowing out the cupcakes. Using a paring knife, cut a concave cone into the top of a cupcake. Insert the tip of the knife into the center of the top of the cupcake, angle the blade toward the outer edge of the top, cut a conical circle of cake, and remove it from the cupcake. Spoon cream filling into the hole. Slice off the top of the cone and place it back on the cupcake to conceal the filling.

How to Give Rolls Amber Crust with Beef Bouillon

WHAT YOU NEED

- Dough
- Greased pan
- Spoon
- 2 beef bouillon cubes
- Measuring cup
- Boiling water
- Pastry brush
- Oven

WHAT TO DO

1. After placing the dough for rolls, shaped into balls, on a greased pan and letting it rise, use a spoon to dissolve two beef bouillon cubes in ¼ cup of boiling water.
2. Using a pastry brush, paint the broth on the rolls.
3. Bake the rolls in the oven.

HOW IT WORKS

When baked, the beef bouillon gives the rolls an amber crust.

THE UPPER CRUST

- To give rolls a top-notch glaze, combine 1 tablespoon of sugar and ¼ cup of milk in a bowl, and use a pastry brush to paint the mixture on the rolls before placing them in the oven.
- To gives rolls a shiny crust, mix one egg beaten with 1 tablespoon of milk, and use a pastry brush to paint the mixture on the rolls before putting them in the oven.

How to Prevent Ice Cream Cone Drips with Peanut Butter

WHAT YOU NEED

- Teaspoon
- Peanut butter, creamy
- Waffle or sugar ice cream cones

WHAT TO DO

1. Place 1 teaspoon of creamy peanut butter in the bottom of a waffle or sugar cone.
2. Add several scoops of ice cream to the cone.

HOW IT WORKS

The peanut butter seals the hole in the bottom of the waffle or sugar cone, stops melted ice cream from leaking through it, and provides a bonus treat at the bottom of the cone.

DON'T SPRING A LEAK

- Other ways to prevent ice cream cone drips: stuff a marshmallow or banana slice in the bottom of a waffle or sugar cone before adding the scoops of ice cream.

- If you coat the inside of a sugar or waffle cone with melted dipping chocolate, the chocolate keeps the cone crispy and prevents the ice cream from leaking from the bottom of the cone.
- To prevent an icy crust from forming on top of an opened carton of ice cream sitting in the freezer, press a piece of waxed paper against the surface of the ice cream before putting the lid back on and returning the container to the freezer.

EVERY TRICK IN THE BOOK
You Scream, I Scream

You can also use an ice cream cone to:

- **Bread Chicken.** Using a food processor, pulverize sugar cones into crumbs, dip chicken tenders in beaten egg, coat with the sugar cone crumbs, and fry.
- **Make Piecrust.** Grind sugar cones in a food processor (or place in a resealable plastic bag and run over with a rolling pin), and press the crumbs into a pie pan.
- **Cook Up S'mores.** Fill a sugar cone with a mixture of chocolate chips and marshmallows, place it on ceramic plate, and heat in a microwave oven for 15 seconds for a gooey treat.
- **Whip Up a Parfait.** Crush sugar cones in a food processor (or place in a resealable plastic bag and run over with a rolling pin), and alternate layers of the crumbs, blueberries, strawberries, and whipped cream in a parfait glass.
- **Create a Yogurt Cone.** Scoop yogurt into a sugar cone and top with slices of fresh fruit, granola, and raisins.
- **Make Granola.** Place some sugar cones in a resealable plastic bag and run over with a rolling pin to grind them into pieces the size of peas, and oats, nuts, and raisins.

How to Stop a Baking Pie from Boiling Over with Pasta

WHAT YOU NEED

- 4 to 8 tubular pasta noodles (macaroni, penne, or ziti)
- Oven

WHAT TO DO

1. Before baking, insert four to six raw tubular pasta noodles (such as macaroni, penne, or ziti) vertically into the center of the top of the piecrust, leaving one end exposed.
2. Bake the pie in the oven as directed.
3. When you're finished baking the pie, remove the noodles.
4. Serve.

HOW IT WORKS

The noodles create vents that allow the fruit filling to release steam, preventing the filling from bursting through the top, boiling over, or making the crust soggy.

EASY AS PIE

To make a flakier piecrust, do any one of the following:

- Substitute sour cream or yogurt for any liquid required by the recipe.
- Substitute vegetable shortening for any butter or margarine called for by the recipe.
- Add a pinch of baking powder to the flour when mixing pie dough.
- Add 1 tablespoon of powdered milk to the flour, use ice-cold water, and add ½ tablespoon of lemon juice.
- To prevent the fruit filling from making the bottom of the piecrust soggy, combine ¼ cup of flour and ½ cup of sugar, and dust the powdery mixture over the bottom of the piecrust before adding the filling.
- To give a pie a glossy top crust, use a pastry brush to paint milk on the top before baking the pie in the oven.
- To prevent the top crust of a pie from browning too quickly in the oven, cut a sheet of brown paper from a grocery bag, spray one side with cooking spray, place it on top of the pie (oil-side down), and lower the oven heat slightly. Five minutes before the pie finishes baking, remove the brown paper.

9

KITCHEN AND FOLK REMEDIES

Whenever I get neck pain, I reach into the panty and grab a clean sock filled with rice and tied shut with a knot.

I heat the sock in the microwave oven for 90 seconds, lie facedown on the carpet, and place the warm sock across the nape of my neck. The rice-filled sock conforms to the shape of my body, stays warm for roughly 30 minutes, and provides penetrating relief.

We've had that sock in our pantry for almost 10 years, we've used it hundreds of times, and we've never needed to replace the rice yet.

Of course, you can go to the store and buy a fancy-schmancy version of my heating pad for $40, but all you're really getting is rice in a sock. And now they're selling heating pads with aromatherapy for $90.

Instead, I grabbed three chamomile tea bags, removed the stringed tag and staple (to avoid putting metal in the microwave oven), and inserted the teabags into my rice-filled sock. Presto! A heating pad with aromatherapy—for the price of three tea bags, a box of rice, and a sock.

How to Soothe Arthritis with Oatmeal

WHAT YOU NEED
- Measuring cup
- 2 cups of instant oatmeal
- 1 cup of water
- Bowl
- Microwave oven

WHAT TO DO
1. Mix 2 cups of instant oatmeal and 1 cup of water in a bowl.
2. Heat the mixture in the microwave oven for 1 minute.
3. Let it cool to the touch, and apply the warm mixture to your hands.

HOW IT WORKS
The warmth of the oatmeal soothes arthritis pain.

SHOW OF HANDS
- Rub mustard over joints afflicted with arthritis. The heat from the mustard provides soothing relieve from arthritis pain.
- For another kitchen remedy for arthritis, mix ¼ teaspoon of Tabasco Pepper Sauce with 2 tablespoons of vegetable shortening, and apply the resulting cream as a salve. The capsaicin in the condiment numbs pain when applied topically.
- Drinking one 8-ounce glass of pineapple juice daily may relieve arthritis pain. Pineapple juice contains the plant enzyme bromelain, which seems to subdue joint inflammation.

How to Eliminate Athlete's Foot with Salt

WHAT YOU NEED
- Footbath
- Warm water
- Salt
- Wooden spoon (optional)
- Towel
- Cornstarch

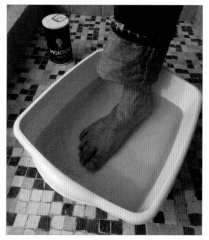

WHAT TO DO
1. To eliminate athlete's foot, fill a footbath with warm water.
2. Dissolve a handful of salt in the water by stirring with your hand or a wooden spoon.
3. Soak each foot in the salty solution for 10 minutes.
4. Dry your feet thoroughly with a towel.
5. Dust your feet and powder the insides of your shoes with cornstarch.
6. Repeat the treatment three times daily until the fungal infection vanishes.

HOW IT WORKS
The salt water creates an inhospitable environment for the fungus, reduces perspiration, and softens the skin. The cornstarch absorbs moisture from your feet, denying fungus a moist breeding ground.

FEET FIRST
A few other ways to help cure athlete's foot:
- Wash your feet with soap and water, dry thoroughly, and then rub liberal amounts of lemon juice over the affected areas. The acids in the lemon juice may sting cracked skin.
- Apply plain yogurt that contains live cultures to the affected area, let dry, rinse clean with warm water, and dry thoroughly. The *Lactobacillus acidophilus* bacteria in the yogurt kill *Tinea pedis*, the fungus responsible for athlete's foot.
- Soak your feet in white vinegar for 10 minutes three times daily until the fungal infection disappears. Or saturate a cotton ball with vinegar and dab the affected areas on your feet. Vinegar is an astringent that kills bacteria and fungus.

How to Soothe a Backache with Rice

WHAT YOU NEED
- Sock
- Rice
- Microwave oven

WHAT TO DO
1. Fill a sock with rice.
2. Tie a knot in the open end of the sock.
3. Heat the rice-filled sock in a microwave oven for 90 seconds.
4. Place the warm, rice-filled sock on your back as a heating pad.
5. Reheat when desired.

HOW IT WORKS
The reusable heating pad conforms to the shape of your back and remains warm for roughly 30 minutes.

WATCH YOUR BACK
Other products you can use to soothe back pain:
- **Vegetable Shortening and Tabasco Pepper Sauce.** Mix 2 tablespoons of vegetable shortening and ¼ teaspoon of Tabasco Pepper Sauce in a small bowl. Massage the homemade salve into your back and sore muscles. The alkaloid capsaicin in the sauce deadens pain when

applied topically. Capsaicin enters nerves and temporarily depletes them of the neurotransmitter that sends pain signals to the brain.

- **Tennis Balls and a Sock.** Insert several tennis balls into a sock, tie a knot at the end, and have a partner roll the sock over your back to massage the sore muscles.

- **Frozen Peas.** Cover a bag of frozen peas with a sheet of paper towel, and place it on your back for up to 20 minutes. The bag of peas conforms to the shape of your back, and the frozen peas act like small ice cubes, constricting the blood vessels and numbing the pain. The paper towel creates a layer of insulation to prevent frostbite. Refreeze the bag of peas for future ice-pack use. Label the bag FOR ICE-PACK USE ONLY. If you want to eat the peas, cook them after they thaw the first time, never after refreezing.

WHEN DO WE EAT?

How to Relieve a Headache

- **Coffee.** Drinking a couple of cups of coffee can reduce a headache. Coffee is a vasoconstrictor, reducing the swelling of blood vessels that cause headache pain.
- **Mustard Powder.** Dissolve 2 teaspoons of mustard powder in a quart of warm water in a footbath, and soak your feet in the solution for 15 minutes. The warmth of the water and mustard draws blood to the feet, easing the pressure on the blood vessels in your head.

- **Pineapple.** Eating a typical serving of pineapple or drinking a glass of pineapple juice reduces the severity and incidence of migraine headaches. Bromelain, the enzyme found only in pineapples, seems to relieve the pain.

How to Relieve a Burn with Mustard

WHAT YOU NEED

- Squeeze bottle of mustard

WHAT TO DO

1. Immediately squeeze mustard over the burn.
2. Gently rub the mustard into the affected area.
3. Let the mustard dry and cake up.
4. Wash off the mustard with cool water.

HOW IT WORKS

Short-order cooks typically embrace this trick to prevent blistering or pain from a burn. At first, the mustard stings briefly, but within moments it eliminates the burning sensation completely.

HOT STUFF

- When wet tea bags are applied directly to the burn or secured in place with gauze, the tannin in the tea relieves the burning sensation.
- Rubbing grape jelly on a mild burn relieves the pain. The jelly moisturizes and cools the skin while the tannin from the grapes soothes the burning sensation.

- Applying honey on burns speeds healing. Honey is hygroscopic and absorbs water, preventing blistering and creating an environment in which disease-producing microorganisms, deprived of their moisture, cannot live. A 2009 study conducted in India and published in the *Indian Journal of Plastic Surgery* concluded that treating a burn with honey also lessens pain, provides rapid sterilization, and reduces scarring.

EVERY TRICK IN THE BOOK
Cut the Mustard

You can also use mustard to:

- **Deodorize Cookware that Smells Like Fish.** Mix 2 tablespoons of mustard powder and ½ cup of water, wash the affected item with the solution, rinse clean, and dry.
- **Salvage Homemade Mayonnaise that Has Begun to Curdle.** Place 1 teaspoon of mustard in a hot bowl, add 1 tablespoon of the curdled mayonnaise at a time, beating with a whisk to re-create the emulsion.

- **Deodorize a Cutting Board.** Dampen the board with water, sprinkle with mustard powder, and scrub with an abrasive sponge. Rinse clean and dry.
- **Flavor and Color Potato Salad.** Add 1 tablespoon of mustard to the mayonnaise before mixing it into the chunked potatoes.
- **Enliven Salad Dressing.** Add 1 teaspoon of mustard to the salad dressing and blend well.
- **Deodorize a Plastic Container.** Fill the container with warm water, dissolve ½ teaspoon of mustard powder, and let sit for 1 hour. Wash with soapy water, rinse clean, and dry.

How to Make Lip Balm with Vegetable Shortening and Kool-Aid

WHAT YOU NEED

- Measuring spoons
- 3 tablespoons of vegetable shortening
- Ceramic coffee mug
- Microwave oven
- 1 packet of Kool-Aid, any flavor
- Spoon
- Clean, empty prescription pill bottle

- Refrigerator

WHAT TO DO

1. Place 3 tablespoons of vegetable shortening in a ceramic coffee cup.
2. Heat the coffee cup in a microwave oven for 1 minute (or until the shortening liquefies).
3. Empty a packet of your favorite flavor of Kool-Aid into the cup of melted shortening.
4. Stir the mixture well with the spoon until the powdered drink mix dissolves in the liquid shortening.
5. Pour the colored liquid into a clean, empty prescription pill bottle.
6. Cap the canister tightly, and refrigerate overnight.
7. In the morning, you've got tasty homemade lip balm.

HOW IT WORKS

Vegetable shortening moisturizes chapped lips, and the powdered drink mix flavors and colors the shortening.

WATCH MY LIPS

- In a pinch, smearing a dab of olive oil on chapped lips relieves the dryness and moisturizes the skin, alleviating the pain.
- Applying a thin coat of honey to chapped lips also moisturizes skin, provided you avoid licking

it off. ***Do not apply honey to the lips of infants under one year of age.*** Honey often carries a benign strain of *C. botulinum*, and an infant's immune system requires 12 months to develop to fight off disease and infection.

- Drinking eight 8-ounce glasses of water daily keeps your lips (and entire body) well hydrated, preventing chapped lips from worsening and accelerating healing.

EVERY TRICK IN THE BOOK

Keeping Your Kool

You can also use Kool-Aid to:

- **Make Virtually Any Color Icing You Desire.** Mix one packet of your choice of any flavor of Kool-Aid drink mix with powdered-sugar icing.
- **Clean an Oven.** Mix the contents of one packet of any flavor of Kool-Aid and 1 cup of water, and use the drink mix like cleanser. The citric acid in the Kool-Aid cuts through the grease and grime in the oven.
- **Make Snow Cones.** In a glass bowl, mix the contents of one envelope of Kool-Aid drink mix, 1 cup of sugar, and ½ cup of cold water. Pour 1 tablespoon of the solution over ½ cup of crushed ice or fresh snow.
- **Flavor and Color Yogurt.** Mix 1 teaspoon of Kool-Aid powdered drink mix into 1 cup of plain yogurt.
- **Dye Hard-Boiled Eggs.** Fill a drinking glass with ⅔ cup of water and the contents of one envelope of Kool-Aid, and stir with a spoon to dissolve. Use a spoon to place a hard-boiled egg  into the solution, keeping the egg submerged until you achieve the desired color. Unlike dying eggs with food coloring, no vinegar is necessary.
- **Make Pancake Syrup.** Mix 1 cup of water, 2 cups of sugar, and the contents of one package of Kool-Aid drink mix in a pot, and boil for 3 minutes.
- **Flavor and Color Applesauce.** Add one 16-ounce packet of red Kool-Aid drink mix to one 15-ounce jar of applesauce, and mix well.

How to Make Cough Syrup with Honey and Olive Oil

WHAT YOU NEED

- Wooden spoon
- Measuring spoons
- Measuring cup
- 4 tablespoons of lemon juice
- 1 cup of clover honey
- ½ cup of olive oil
- Saucepan
- Stove
- Airtight container

WHAT TO DO

1. Using the wooden spoon, mix the lemon juice, honey, and olive oil in a saucepan.
2. Warm the mixture over low heat on the stove for 5 minutes.
3. Stir vigorously for several minutes until the mixture attains the consistency of syrup.
4. Store the homemade cough syrup in an airtight container.
5. To relieve a cough, take 1 teaspoon of the formula every 2 hours. **Do not feed honey to an infant under one year of age.** Honey often carries a benign strain of *C. botulinum*, and an infant's immune system requires 12 months to develop to fight off disease and infection.

HOW IT WORKS

The mildly antibiotic honey soothes the throat, relieves coughing, and acts as a sedative to the nervous system.

EVERY TRICK IN THE BOOK
Honey Do

You can also use honey to:

- **Enhance Sautéed Onions.** Add a little honey to the butter.
- **Sweeten Boiled Potatoes.** Add 1 tablespoon of honey to the cooking water.
- **Give Yourself a Luxurious Facial Treatment.** Mix up 1 cup of warm oatmeal, add enough honey to thicken, let cool to the touch, and apply the mixture to your dry face.

How to Disinfect a Wound with Honey

WHAT YOU NEED
- Soap
- Water
- Honey
- Sterile gauze pads (or maxi pads)
- Adhesive tape

WHAT TO DO
1. Clean the laceration or abrasion with soap and water.
2. Apply honey directly on sterile gauze pad (or maxi pad), and then place the pad on the wound. Use a 4-inch square pad for every 1 ounce of honey used.
3. If using a gauze pad, place a second gauze pad on top of the first dressing, and secure it in place with adhesive tape. Or secure the maxi pad in place with adhesive tape.
4. Changing the dressing once daily (or more frequently if necessary) if fluid oozes from the wound. If no fluid oozes from the wound, change the honey and dressing once every five days.

HOW IT WORKS
Applying honey to a laceration or abrasion as an ointment disinfects the wound, kills bacteria, and hastens healing. Honey is hygroscopic and absorbs water, creating an environment that destroys disease-producing microorganisms by sucking the moisture from their cells. Honey also contains dozens of antioxidants, minerals, enzymes, amino acids, fats, and compounds that help kill microbes and expedite healing.

BAD BLOOD
- In an emergency, applying flour to a laceration helps the blood clot, giving you time to get to a doctor.
- To stop minor bleeding from a cut, dampen a tea bag with warm water, and press it over the wound. The tannin does the trick.
- Pouring Listerine antiseptic mouthwash (original flavor) over a laceration or abrasion disinfects the cuts and scrapes.
- Squeezing juice from a fresh lemon on a cut or applying lemon juice with a cotton ball disinfects the wound.

How to Give Yourself a Facial with Applesauce

WHAT YOU NEED

- Towel
- Applesauce
- Warm water
- Cool water
- Soft, clean towel

WHAT TO DO

1. Lie down with a towel under your head and shoulders.
2. Gently coat your face with applesauce, avoiding your eyes.
3. Wait 30 minutes.
4. Wash the applesauce from your face with warm water, followed by cool water.
5. Pat your face dry with a soft, clean towel.

HOW IT WORKS

The malic acid in the applesauce helps exfoliate dead skin cells, leaving your face smooth and soft. The applesauce cleans dry skin, and the pectin in the applesauce absorbs excess oil. The warm water opens the pores, and the cool water closes the pores.

IN YOUR FACE

You can also give yourself a facial with:

- **Powdered Milk.** Mix ¼ cup of powdered milk with enough water to make a thick paste. Apply the milky paste to your face, let dry, then wash off. The lactic acid removes grime and exfoliates dead skin, and the proteins in the milk leave the skin feeling silky smooth.

- **Rolled Oats and Honey.** Mix up 1 cup of warm oatmeal, add enough honey to thicken, let cool to the touch, and then apply to your dry face. Wait 10 minutes, and then rinse with warm water. The warmth and the honey draw the oil from your skin, and the oatmeal absorbs it.

- **Salt and Olive Oil.** To give yourself a revitalizing facial, mix equal parts salt and olive oil, wash your face, apply warm, wet washcloths to your face to open the pores, and then apply the pasty solution, massaging the face with long upward and inward strokes for 5 minutes. Remove the concoction, and rinse your face clean with warm water, followed by cool water.

- **Toothpaste.** Squeeze a dollop of toothpaste into the cupped palm of your hand, add a few drops of water, and rub your hands together to create a lather. Coat your face with the toothpaste lather, then rinse thoroughly. Toothpaste is a mild abrasive that cleanses the skin and leaves your face feeling minty fresh.

EVERY TRICK IN THE BOOK
An Apple a Day

You can also use applesauce to:

- **Substitute for Butter, Margarine, or Oil in a Cake Mix.** Use an equal amount of applesauce for the butter, margarine, or oil listed in the recipe.

- **Reduce the Calories and Fat in Home-Baked Goods.** When mixing up the dough or batter, substitute the same amount of applesauce for the oil called for by the recipe.

- **Make Pills Easier to Swallow.** If you have difficulty swallowing pills, use a mortar and pestle to crush up the pills and mix the powder into applesauce.

- **Clean Mirrors.** Smear applesauce on the glass, and then wipe clean.

How to Relieve Food Poisoning with Sugar, Lemon, and Salt

WHAT YOU NEED

- Measuring spoons
- 3 teaspoons of sugar
- 2 teaspoons of lemon juice
- 1 teaspoon of salt
- Tall drinking glass
- Water
- Spoon

WHAT TO DO

1. Add 3 teaspoons of sugar, 2 teaspoons of lemon juice, and 1 teaspoon of salt to a tall glass of water.
2. Using a spoon, mix well.
3. Drink the solution.

HOW IT WORKS

This homemade rehydrating solution replaces the glucose, minerals, and vitamin C being flushed out of your body during a bout of diarrhea and vomiting.

WHAT'S YOUR POISON?

- Here's another recipe for a rehydrating solution that replenishes electrolytes lost during a bout with diarrhea: 1 cup of apple juice, 3 tablespoons of honey, 1 teaspoon of salt, and 2 cups of water. The apple juice provides potassium, the honey supplies glucose, and the salt furnishes sodium. Drink the solution throughout the day or as needed.
- Drinking flat ginger ale helps settle an upset stomach. The ginger seems to relax the stomach muscles.
- Another way to replace the liquids, salts, and minerals depleted by diarrhea: sip 1 cup of chicken bouillon.
- When you feel ready to eat solid foods again, start with bland, easily digestible foods like saltine crackers, applesauce, rice, toast, and Popsicles.

How to Cure Hiccups with a Paper Cup

WHAT YOU NEED
- Paper cup
- Water

WHAT TO DO
1. Fill a paper cup with water, and place the cup on a countertop.
2. Insert your index fingers into your ears.
3. Using the thumb and pinkie finger of each hand, pick up the paper cup, hold your breath, and gulp down the water.

HOW IT WORKS
This unusual technique tames the spasms in your diaphragm by increasing carbon dioxide levels, temporarily immobilizing the diaphragm, and distracting your mind. The British medical journal the *Lancet* claims that sticking your fingers in your ears temporarily short-circuits the vagus nerve, which controls the hiccups.

OTHER HICCUP CURES
- **Pineapple Juice.** Drink a glass of pineapple juice. The acidity seems to relieve the hiccups.
- **Sugar.** Swallow 1 teaspoon of sugar without drinking any water. The texture of the sugar seems reprogram the nerve receptors that control the diaphragm.
- **Apple Cider Vinegar.** Many people cure hiccups by drinking 1 teaspoon of apple cider vinegar stirred into 1 cup of warm water.
- **Peanut Butter.** The act of chewing, swallowing, and clearing the mouth of 1 heaping teaspoon of creamy peanut butter interrupts breathing patterns, recalibrating the diaphragm to stop the spasms.
- **Dill Seeds.** Chewing and swallowing 1 teaspoon of dill seeds seems to stimulate the vagus nerve, curing hiccups.
- **Lemon Juice.** Swallowing a spoonful of lemon juice can shock the nerves of the diaphragm, bringing the spasms to a halt.

How to Soothe a Bee or Wasp Sting with Meat Tenderizer

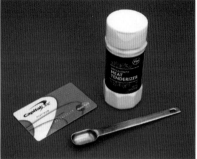

WHAT YOU NEED

- Credit card
- Measuring spoons
- ½ teaspoon of meat tenderizer (containing papain)
- 2 teaspoons of water

WHAT TO DO

1. Remove the stinger and venom sack from the affected area by using the edge of a credit card to lightly scrape the skin to flick it away.
2. Mix ½ teaspoon of meat tenderizer and 2 teaspoons of water into a paste.
3. Apply the paste to the affected area.
4. Let sit for up to 30 minutes.
5. Wash clean with warm water.

HOW IT WORKS

The enzyme papain, found in unripe papaya fruit, digests the proteins in the venom, reducing inflammation and pain.

WHAT'S BUGGING YOU?

- To repel bees and wasps (mosquitoes too), tie a sheet of Bounce fabric softener through a belt loop or the plastic flap in the back of a baseball cap. Oleander, the fragrance in Bounce Outdoor Fresh, repels insects.
- Pop open a can of beer, pour out ¼ of the beer, and tie a loop of dental floss through the flip-top lid of the can. Hang the open beer can from a fence post or tree branch wherever wasps are giving you trouble. Wasps love beer. They fly into the can, drink the beer, get drunk, and drown.

- Fill a 16-ounce trigger-spray bottle with vodka and spray the bees or wasps. The alcohol in vodka kills bees and wasps instantly, and you can celebrate, if so inclined, with the leftover vodka.

How to Soothe Itchy Skin with Oatmeal and Panty Hose

WHAT YOU NEED
- Blender
- Measuring cup
- 1 cup of rolled oats
- Scissors
- Clean, used pair of panty hose
- Bathtub
- Warm water

WHAT TO DO
1. Using a blender, grind 1 cup of rolled oats into a fine powder.
2. Using a pair of scissors, cut off the foot from a clean, used pair of panty hose.
3. Fill with the powdered oats, and tie a knot in the nylon.
4. Tie the oatmeal sachet to the spigot of the bathtub, letting it dangle in the flow of water as the tub fills with warm water.
5. Soak for 30 minutes in this inexpensive and soothing oatmeal bath.
6. Repeat whenever necessary.

HOW IT WORKS
As an astringent, oatmeal soothes the skin, relieves itching, and contains beneficial proteins. Oatmeal also cleans the pores and kills bacteria.

SCRATCHING THE SURFACE
- Soak for 10 minutes in a warm bath, and then add 1 teaspoon of olive oil to the water and soak for another 5 minutes. The warm water softens scaly patches of skin and soothes the itching, and the oil seals the moisture in your skin.
- Dissolve ½ cup of baking soda in a tepid bath. Soak in the bath for 15 minutes.
- To remedy dry, itchy skin, rub mayonnaise into the affected area and let sit for 15 minutes. The oil and vinegar in the mayonnaise moisturize and rejuvenate the dry skin and relieve the itch.
- Sprinkle cornstarch on the rash and rub into the skin to absorb moisture and relieve the itching.

How to Relieve an Ulcer with Cranberry Juice

WHAT YOU NEED
- Drinking glass, 8-ounce
- Cranberry juice

WHAT TO DO
1. Fill the drinking glass with cranberry juice.
2. Drink the contents of the glass.
3. Repeat daily.

HOW IT WORKS
A 2005 study at the Beijing Institute for Cancer Research found that drinking one cup of cranberry juice daily eliminates *Helicobacter pylori*, the bacterium that causes stomach ulcers. Five years earlier, a study at Technion and Tel Aviv University found preliminary evidence that proanthocyanidins in cranberry juice may inhibit *H. pylori* from attaching to the stomach lining and causing an ulcer. The study also suggested that cranberry juice causes attached *H. pylori* to release their grip on the stomach lining.

GOING BELLY UP
- Most ulcers in the stomach or duodenum (the uppermost section of the small intestine) are caused by a bacterium called *H. pylori* that eats through the thick layer of mucus lining of the stomach or duodenum. Pepsin, a digestive enzyme, then seeps into the openings, digesting the body's tissue and causing burning pain.
- Antibiotics can cure most ulcers caused by *H. pylori*.
- Long-term use of nonsteroidal anti-inflammatory drugs (such as aspirin and ibuprofen) can also cause ulcers.
- Contrary to popular belief, spicy food and stress do not cause ulcers. They may, however, aggravate ulcer symptoms in some people.
- Ulcers tend to act up when the stomach is empty and subside again after eating food.
- To reduce ulcer pain, drink eight 8-ounce glasses of water daily. The water dilutes the acids in the stomach, lessening discomfort.

10

CLEANING TRICKS

One night I found my wife, Debbie, standing in our kitchen in tears. She had filled a brand-new pot with water, placed it on a hot burner, and forgotten about it. The water boiled out of the pot, leaving a dark brown burn stain inside the pot.

"I'm sorry," she said. "I guess we have to throw it out."

I reminded her that I write these books for a living. "Leave it to me," I said.

I filled the pot with water, dropped in four denture cleansing tablets, and let the pot sit in the sink overnight. In the morning, I grabbed a sponge and gently wiped the inside of the pot. The burn stain came right out—without any elbow grease whatsoever.

"Thank you for saving our new pot," said Debbie.

"I'm sorry," I said.

"What for?"

"I forgot to toss my dentures in the pot last night. I could have killed two birds with one stone."

"But you don't wear dentures."

"Sorry, I forgot that too."

How to Clean a Barbecue Grill with Aluminum Foil

WHAT YOU NEED
- Oven mitt
- Sheet of aluminum foil

WHAT TO DO

1. Immediately after you finish barbecuing, put on an oven mitt and carefully place a sheet of aluminum foil with the shiny side facing down on the hot grill.
2. Close the lid.
3. The next time you plan to use the barbecue, open the lid and gently peel off the aluminum foil.
4. Crumple the sheet into a ball, and use it to scrub the grill clean.

HOW IT WORKS
The hot grill heats up the aluminum foil, allowing the burned-on food to lift off the grill and attach itself to the foil. The abrasive foil ball scrubs the grill clean.

NOW YOU'RE COOKING
A few other ways to clean a barbecue grill rack:
- Use the method presented in "How to Clean Oven Racks with Ammonia" on page 62.
- Mix equal parts baking soda and water to make a thick paste, apply to the cool rack with a wire brush, and scrub. Wipe clean, and dry with a clean cloth.
- Mix ½ cup of dishwashing liquid and 1 gallon of water in a bucket. Using a sponge, apply the soapy solution to the cool rack, scrub with a wire brush, and rinse clean.
- Place the cool rack on the ground outside, and, wearing protective eyewear, a respirator mask, and rubber gloves, coat the rack with oven cleaner. Let sit for 1 hour, and then rinse well with a garden hose.

How to Remove Candle Wax from a Tablecloth with a Clothes Iron

WHAT YOU NEED

- Credit card
- Paper towel
- Ironing board
- Clothes iron

WHAT TO DO

1. To remove candle wax from a tablecloth, use the edge of a credit card to scrape off as much wax as possible.
2. Place a sheet of paper towel on the ironing board cover.
3. Place the tablecloth on the ironing board, positioning the wax stain over the paper towel.
4. Place a second sheet of paper towel on top of the wax stain.
5. With a clothes iron set on warm, gently and carefully press the paper towel.

HOW IT WORKS

The heat from the clothes iron melts the wax, and the paper towel absorbs the liquefied wax.

A DIFFERENT BALL OF WAX

- To clean candle wax stains from linen, saturate the spot with vegetable oil, blot up the excess oil with a paper towel, and launder as usual.
- To clean candle wax from a wood floor, heat the wax with a blow-dryer set on warm, and then wipe clean with a paper towel.
- To remove stubborn candle wax from a wood floor or wood furniture, rub a dollop of mayonnaise into the wax, let sit for 5 minutes, and wipe clean with a soft cloth.

EVERY TRICK IN THE BOOK
Ironing Out the Wrinkles

You can also use a clothes iron to:

- **Make a Grilled Cheese Sandwich.** Wrap a cheese sandwich in aluminum foil, and iron each side for 20 seconds.
- **Clean a Melted Plastic Bag from a Glass Cooktop.** When the cooktop cools to room temperature, cover the melted plastic with a sheet of waxed paper, and gently press the waxed paper with a clothes iron set on warm. When the heat from the clothes iron softens the plastic, remove the waxed paper, and use a single-edge razor blade to carefully scrape off the remaining plastic.
- **Remove Chewing Gum from Wood Furniture.** Place a sheet of paper towel over the gum, and press the paper towel with a warm clothes iron. The heat from the clothes iron melts the gum, and the paper towel absorbs it.
- **Raise Indentations from Carpet.** If you move a sofa or coffee table, leaving dents in the carpet, place a damp cloth over the crater, and using the steam setting, run the clothes iron over the cloth for 30 seconds. Then use a stiff hairbrush or your fingers to lift the carpet fibers.
- **Clean Crayon Marks or Grease Stains from Walls.** Place a sheet of paper towel over the crayon marks or grease stains, and press gently with a warm clothes iron. The heat from the clothes iron melts the wax or grease, and the paper towel absorbs it.

How to Clean Baked-On Food from a Casserole Dish with Denture Cleanser

WHAT YOU NEED
- Water
- 2 or 3 denture cleansing tablets
- Sponge

WHAT TO DO
1. Fill the stained casserole dish with water.
2. Drop in two or three denture cleansing tablets.
3. Let the casserole dish sit undisturbed overnight.
4. In the morning, wipe the casserole dish clean with a sponge.
5. Rinse with water and dry.

HOW IT WORKS
The effervescent action of the denture cleansing tablets loosens the baked-on food from the casserole dish.

WHEN DO WE EAT?
How to Shine Stainless-Steel Appliances

Stainless steel, an iron alloy containing more than 10 percent chromium, captures fingerprints—notoriously well.

To clean stainless steel, first you have to remove those finger-prints. Dampen a clean, soft cloth with warm water, club soda, or rubbing alcohol, and wipe the appliance clean. If necessary, use a few drops of mild dishwashing liquid in a bucket of warm water, and rinse well.

Never use an abrasive cleanser or bleach to scrub stainless steel. An abrasive may remove the oxide coating that protects the stainless steel from rust. Bleach damages the finish.

To give those appliances a beautiful shine, put a few drops of baby oil (food-safe mineral oil), olive oil, or a dab of petroleum jelly on a soft, clean cloth, and rub it into the metal. Then use a second soft, clean cloth to buff—going with the grain of the finish, not circular motions—to achieve a glimmering shine.

EVERY TRICK IN THE BOOK

Sink Your Teeth into It

You can also use denture cleansing tablets to:

- **Clean Stains from Inside a Microwave Oven.** Dissolve two denture cleansing tablets in a glass of water. Using a sponge, apply the solution to the inside of the microwave oven, and let sit for 5 minutes. Rinse clean with a clean sponge and water.
- **Clean Stove Burner Drip Plates.** Fill the kitchen sink with water, add four denture cleansing tablets, and let the drip plates soak in the solution overnight. Rinse clean.
- **Remove Mineral Deposits from an Electric Teakettle.** Fill the kettle with enough water to cover the heating element, add four denture cleansing tablets, and let sit overnight. In the morning, scrub with a bristle bottlebrush, and rinse clean with hot water.
- **Clean the Inside of a Vase, Glass Bottle, Water Bottle, or Thermos Bottle.** Fill the item with water, drop in two denture cleansing tablets, and let sit for 1 hour. Rinse clean.

- **Erase Stains from a China Teacup or Coffee Mug.** Fill the cup or mug with water, add one denture cleansing tablet, and let sit overnight. In the morning, wash clean, rinse, and dry.
- **Clean the Inside of a Glass Coffeepot.** Fill the coffeepot with water, drop in two denture cleansing tablets, let sit overnight, and rinse clean.
- **Remove Scorch Marks from a Pot or Pan.** Fill the cookware with water, add two to three denture cleansing tablets, and let sit overnight. In the morning, wash with soapy water, rinse clean, and dry thoroughly.

How to Scrub a Cast-Iron Pan with Salt

WHAT YOU NEED

- Oven
- Stove
- Measuring cup
- Salt
- Wooden spoon
- Dishwashing liquid
- Hot water
- Dish towel
- Vegetable oil (or shortening)
- Soft cloth (or paper towel)

WHAT TO DO

1. Preheat the oven to 300° Fahrenheit.
2. To clean grease and grime from inside a cast-iron pan, carefully heat the pan on a stove burner set on high.
3. When the pan starts smoking, pour 1 cup of salt into the pan, and use a wooden spoon to push the salt around the pan to better absorb any grease and grime.
4. When the salt starts turning gray, discard it.
5. If the surface of the pan does not appear dull, repeat the salt treatment.
6. Wash the pan clean with hot soapy water (made with mild dishwashing liquid), rinse clean, and dry thoroughly with a dish towel.
7. Dry the pan in the preheated oven for 20 minutes.
8. Turn off the oven, and let the cast-iron pan sit in the oven until it cools to room temperature.
9. Apply a thin, even coat of vegetable oil (or shortening) to the inside and outside of the pan (including the lid) with a soft cloth or paper towel.

HOW IT WORKS

Salt, being highly absorbent, soaks up the grease and grime from the heated cast-iron pan.

How to Clean a Glass Cooktop with a Credit Card and Toothpaste

WHAT YOU NEED

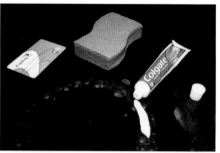

- Old credit card
- Toothpaste (ideally containing baking soda)
- Abrasive sponge
- Water
- Clean, soft dish towel

WHAT TO DO

1. To clean stubborn, baked-on food from a glass or smooth ceramic cooktop, let the cooktop cool to room temperature.
2. Use the edge of an old credit card to gently scrape off the gunk.
3. Rub a liberal dollop of toothpaste into the stains. Let sit for 5 minutes.
4. Scrub the toothpaste with the dry, abrasive sponge.
5. Let sit for another 5 minutes.
6. Dampen the sponge with water and continue scrubbing.
7. Add more toothpaste to any stubborn stains, and scrub further, rinsing the sponge if desired.
8. Rinse well, and dry with a clean, soft dish towel.

HOW IT WORKS

The mild abrasives in the toothpaste scrub baked-on food from the stovetop, and the toothpaste leaves your stove smelling minty fresh.

CLEAN SWEEP

Other ways to clean grease from a stovetop:

- Make a thick paste from baking soda and water, apply the paste to the surface, and let sit for 1 hour to give the baking soda sufficient time to absorb the grease. Rinse clean and dry thoroughly.
- Sprinkle salt over a hot spill on a stovetop, let cool, and scrape clean with a sponge. The salt absorbs the grease and acts as a mild abrasive to help scour the mess.
- Spray the baked-on grease with stain remover, let sit for 5 minutes, and wipe clean.
- Dampen a sponge with white vinegar, scrub clean, and buff dry with a soft, clean cloth. Vinegar shines and deodorizes stovetops.

How to Clean a Copper Pot with Ketchup

WHAT YOU NEED
- Ketchup
- Water
- Abrasive sponge (optional)

WHAT TO DO
1. Squeeze ketchup directly from the bottle to cover the tarnish on the copper pot.
2. Let sit for 15 minutes.
3. Rinse clean under running water, scrubbing the copper with an abrasive sponge if desired.
4. Repeat if necessary.

HOW IT WORKS
The acids from the tomatoes and vinegar dissolve the tarnish.

BOTTOMS UP
Some other ways to clean stubborn stains and tarnish from copper pots:
- Mix equal parts flour and salt and add enough white vinegar to make a paste. Spread a thick coat of this paste on the copper, let dry, then rinse and wipe clean.
- Mix 2 tablespoons of lemon juice and 1 tablespoon of salt, and rub the mixture into the tarnished copper. The chemical reaction cleans the cooper instantly. Rinse clean and dry.
- Rub toothpaste over the tarnish, let sit for 10 minutes, rinse clean, and dry.
- Mix four parts white vinegar and to one part salt in a bowl, dampen a sponge with the solution, and gently rub the copper. Wash, rinse, and dry.

How to Sanitize a Countertop with Shaving Cream

WHAT YOU NEED

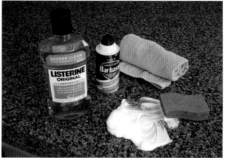

- Shaving cream
- Sponge
- Water
- Soft cloth
- Listerine antiseptic mouthwash
- Clean dish towel

WHAT TO DO

1. Spray a large dollop of shaving cream on a dirty countertop.
2. With your bare hand, rub the shaving cream all over the countertop.
3. Rinse clean with a damp sponge.
4. Saturate a sponge with Listerine antiseptic mouthwash and wipe down the surface.
5. Let the mouthwash sit undisturbed on the countertop for 10 minutes.
6. Rinse clean with a damp sponge.
7. Dry the countertop with a clean dish towel.

HOW IT WORKS

The condensed soap and emollients in the shaving cream cleans stubborn grease and grime from the countertop. The antibacterial Listerine, developed as an antiseptic for use in surgical procedures, sanitizes the countertop.

EVERY TRICK IN THE BOOK

Close Shave

You can also use shaving cream to:

- **Defog a Mirror.** Fill your cupped palm with shaving cream, rub it over the entire surface of the mirror, and wipe clean with a soft cloth (without using any water). The thin film of soap and emollients left behind prevent the mirror from steaming up.
- **Clean Ketchup, Spaghetti Sauce, or Red Wine Stains from Carpet.** After using club soda to blot up as much of the stain as possible, spray a dab of shaving cream on the spot, rub it into the spot with your fingers, and blot clean with a damp, clean cloth.
- **Mousse Your Hair.** A dab of shaving cream doubles as hair gel.

How to Wash Pots and Pans with Panty Hose

WHAT YOU NEED

- Scissors
- Clean, used pair of panty hose

WHAT TO DO

1. Using a pair of scissors, cut off the two legs from a clean, used pair of panty hose.
2. Snip off the foot from one of those legs at the ankle, and set it aside.
3. Tie knots along each leg as close together as possible—creating two wads of knots.
4. Stuff the two knotted legs into the empty foot you previously set aside.
5. Tie a knot in the open end of the foot.
6. Use the sachet to scrub pots and pans.

HOW IT WORKS

The abrasive nylon doubles as a scratchless and effective scrubber for cleaning pots and pans.

DISHING THE DIRT

To make homemade scouring powder, mix 1 cup of baking soda, 1 cup of borax, and 1 cup of salt, and store the mixture in an airtight container, labeled appropriately with an indelible marker. Keep the homemade cleanser out of reach of children and pets.

How to Unclog a Drain with Jell-O

WHAT YOU NEED

- Glass mixing bowl
- Whisk
- 1 package of Jell-O, 3 ounces
- Measuring cup
- Boiling water
- 1 cup of white vinegar
- Refrigerator
- Sticky note
- Pen or pencil

WHAT TO DO

1. In a glass mixing bowl and using the whisk, dissolve one 3-ounce package of Jell-O in 1 cup of boiling water.
2. Add 1 cup of white vinegar.
3. Mix well with the whisk to dissolve all the powder.
4. Let gel in refrigerator.
5. Place a sticky note on the bowl to prevent anyone from accidentally eating the vinegar-laced Jell-O.
6. Slowly pour the vinegar Jell-O down the drain, and let sit overnight.
7. In the morning, flush the drain with boiling water to wash away the Jell-O and any remaining debris.

HOW IT WORKS

The acetic acid in vinegar can dissolve a clogged drain; however, if you pour vinegar down a clogged drain, the vinegar will seep down the pipe before it has enough time to eat away the wad of grease and debris. The gelatin mixture gives the acetic acid sufficient time to sit in the pipes to dissolve the clog.

DOWN THE DRAIN

Other ways to clear a clogged drain:

- If you haven't poured any commercial drain cleaner down the drain and no water stands in the sink, pour 1 cup of baking soda down the drain. Heat 1 cup of white vinegar in the microwave oven for 2 minutes, and pour it down the drain. Allow the baking soda and vinegar to react for 10 minutes, giving the bubbling action time to break down any grease. Pour a kettle of boiling water down the drain to flush out the dislodged grease.
- To use a blow dryer to fix a clogged sink, see page 42.

- Dissolve four denture cleansing tablets in 2 cups of water, pour the mixture into the clogged drain, and let sit overnight to loosen any grease in the trap. In the morning, flush with hot water.
- Provided you haven't poured any commercial drain cleaner down the drain and no water stands in the sink, pour 2 cups of bleach down the drain, and let sit overnight. The bleach saturates and softens any coagulated grease or debris in the trap. In the morning, run the hot water for 3 minutes to flush the debris through the pipes. (Do not let bleach drip or puddle on stainless steel.)

EVERY TRICK IN THE BOOK
The Joy of Jell-O

You can also use gelatin to:

- **Add Fruit Flavor to Angel Food Cake.** Substitute 1 packet of any flavor Jell-O for the equal amount of sugar called for by the recipe.
- **Enhance Cream Cheese.** After spreading the cream cheese on a bagel, English muffin, or slice of toast, sprinkle it with one or two pinches of flavored Jell-O powder.
- **Perk Up Mousse.** Dissolve 1 tablespoon of any flavor Jell-O powder in 1 tablespoon of cold water, add to the recipe, and chill the mousse before serving.
- **Enliven Apple Pie.** Before adding the top crust to an apple pie, sprinkle ¼ cup of any flavor Jell-O powder over the apple filling.

How to Wipe Up a Dropped Egg with Salt

WHAT YOU NEED
- Salt
- Paper towel

WHAT TO DO
1. If you accidentally drop an egg on the kitchen floor, pick up the eggs shells and discard.
2. Cover the spill with a mountain of salt.
3. Let sit for 10 to 15 minutes so the salt can absorb the egg.
4. Pick up the mess with a sheet of paper towel.

HOW IT WORKS
The salt, being highly absorbent, absorbs the egg white and yolk, which can then easily be swept up with a paper towel.

WHEN DO WE EAT?
More Ways to Get the Best Eggs

- Always purchase eggs from a refrigerated case, bring them home quickly, and refrigerate immediately in the coldest section of the refrigerator. Eggs stored at room temperature lose their quality rapidly and should be discarded after 2 hours.
- Eggs stored in the carton remain fresh longer than eggs stored in the refrigerator egg shelf. The snug carton prevents the eggs from losing moisture and absorbing odors from the refrigerator.
- To keep eggs fresh, rub vegetable oil over the entire shell to seal the pores closed.
- To prevent the spread of bacteria, wash your hands, utensils, and equipment and work surfaces thoroughly with hot, soapy water for at least 20 seconds before and after handling eggs.

How to Deodorize a Lunch Box with a Slice of Bread

WHAT YOU NEED
- 1 slice of white bread
- Vinegar
- Dishwashing liquid
- Water
- Dish towel

WHAT TO DO
1. To deodorize a stinky metal or plastic lunch box, place a slice of white bread in the lunch box.
2. Dampen the bread with white vinegar.
3. Seal the lunch box shut.
4. Let sit overnight.
5. In the morning, open the lunch box and discard the soggy bread.
6. Wash the lunch box with soapy water made with dishwashing liquid.
7. Rinse clean, and dry with a dish towel.

HOW IT WORKS
The vinegar neutralizes odors, and the white bread absorbs them.

LET'S DO LUNCH
- If you store a sandwich in a resealable plastic bag in the freezer overnight and place it in a lunch box first thing in the morning, the sandwich will thaw by lunchtime. Make a week's worth of sandwiches at a time, store them in the freezer, and add one to the lunch box each morning.
- Use clean, empty pill bottles to store salad dressing, ketchup, or mustard.
- Place a thermos bottle inside a clean, old sock for protection.
- Use a frozen juice box as an ice pack in the lunch box to keep the food fresh. The juice will thaw by lunchtime.

EVERY TRICK IN THE BOOK

Boxed In

You can also use a lunch box to:

- **Store Hair Accessories.** Hair brushes, combs, scrunchies, and barrettes fit nicely inside a lunch box.
- **Store Cosmetics.** A lunch box makes a convenient carrying case for storing makeup.
- **Store Crayons.** Not only can crayons and other craft materials be stored in a lunch box, but the handle makes carrying them around a snap.

- **Store Costume Jewelry.** Keep bangles and necklaces inside a lunch box for easy access and simple organization of a kid's room.
- **Store Tools.** A discarded lunch box makes an excellent toolbox, just large enough to hold small tools.

WHEN DO WE EAT?

How to Clean a Thermos Bottle

Any of the following household products can be used to clean a thermos bottle:

- **Baking Soda.** Fill the bottle with warm water, add 2 tablespoons of baking soda, seal the lid, and shake well. Let sit for 10 minutes.
- **Bleach.** Fill the bottle with warm water, add 1 teaspoon of bleach, seal the lid, and shake well. Let sit for 1 hour. Wash and rinse well.
- **Denture Cleanser.** Fill the bottle with water, add two denture cleansing tables, and let sit overnight. In the morning, drain and wash clean.

- **Rice and Vinegar.** Pour ½ cup of rice and ½ cup white vinegar into the bottle. Seal the lid, and shake vigorously for 3 minutes, allowing the grains of rice to scrub the inside walls of the bottle. Drain, and wash with soapy water.
- **Salt.** Fill the bottle with warm water, add 1 tablespoon of salt, seal the lid, and shake well to dissolve the salt. Let sit overnight, and in the morning, wash with soapy water.

How to Neutralize Kitchen Odors with Vinegar

WHAT YOU NEED
- Drinking glass
- White vinegar

WHAT TO DO
1. To eliminate the smell of fish, broccoli, cabbage, and other pungent foods from the kitchen, fill a drinking glass halfway with white vinegar.
2. Set the glass of vinegar on the kitchen counter.

HOW IT WORKS
Vinegar is a natural deodorizer. In 5 minutes, the vinegar neutralizes the feisty odors.

A BREATH OF FRESH AIR
You can also use these other great deodorizers:

- **Cinnamon.** Sprinkle 1 teaspoon of ground cinnamon in a saucepan and warm it up on the stove to cover up the smell of burned food in the kitchen.
- **Coffee.** Fill a bowl with fresh coffee grounds and place it on the kitchen counter. The coffee grounds absorb foul cooking odors.

- **Lemon Juice.** Boil 1 tablespoon of lemon juice in a saucepan for 3 minutes to mask the smell of burned foods from the kitchen.
- **Tea.** Brew a pot of tea, let cool to room temperature, and pour it into a 16-ounce trigger spray bottle. Spray the tea around the house. Tea is a natural air freshener.

How to Clean Silverware with Baking Soda and Aluminum Foil

WHAT YOU NEED

- Metal cake pan
- Aluminum foil
- Bowl
- Measuring spoons
- 4 tablespoons of baking soda
- Measuring cups
- 2 quarts of water
- Cooking thermometer
- Stove

WHAT TO DO

1. Line the bottom of the metal cake pan with one or two sheets of aluminum foil.
2. In a bowl, dissolve 4 tablespoons of baking soda in 2 quarts of water.
3. Pour just enough of the solution into the pan so when you add the silverware later, the solution will cover the silverware.
4. Using the cooking thermometer, heat the water on the stove above 150° Fahrenheit—but do not let the water boil.
5. Place the tarnished silverware in the pan so it rests on the aluminum foil.
6. Let the silverware soak over the heat for 10 minutes, the turn off the heat, and let the water cool before removing the silverware.

HOW IT WORKS

Silver gradually darkens because silver chemically reacts with sulfur-containing substances in the air to form silver sulfide, which is black. This cleaning technique creates a chemical reaction that converts the silver sulfide back into silver—without removing any of the silver from the utensils. Like silver, aluminum forms compounds with sulfur—but with a greater affinity than silver. The hydrogen produced from heating the baking soda transfers the sulfur from the silver to the aluminum, creating aluminum sulfide, which adheres to the aluminum foil or forms tiny yellow flakes in the bottom of the pan.

THE SILVER LINING

- The silver and aluminum must be in contact with each other during this cleaning method because a small electric current flows between them during the reaction.
- Polishing silverware with an abrasive cleanser removes the silver sulfide and some of the silver from the surface. Other chemical tarnish-removers dissolve the silver sulfide but also remove some of the silver.

EVERY TRICK IN THE BOOK

The Old Brush Off

You can also use toothpaste to:

- **Clean Silverware.** Instead of using expensive silver polish, rub regular-flavor toothpaste on the silverware, and then rub it off with a paper towel. Rinse clean and dry.
- **Shine a Chrome or Plastic Toaster.** Unplug the appliance, squeeze a dollop of toothpaste on a damp sponge, and scrub. Rinse clean and dry.
- **Clean the Smell of Fish, Garlic, or Onions from Your Hands.** Squeeze a dollop of toothpaste into the palm of your hand, rub your hands together under running water, and rinse clean.
- **Clean Stains from China, Coffee Mugs, or Tea Cups.** Squeeze a dab of toothpaste on a soft, clean cloth and gently rub the stains. Rinse clean and dry.

How to Sanitize a Kitchen Sponge with Bleach

WHAT YOU NEED

- Measuring cups
- ¾ cup of bleach
- 1 gallon of water
- Bowl

WHAT TO DO

1. To kill all the germs breeding in your kitchen sponge, mix ¾ cup of bleach in 1 gallon of water in a bowl.
2. Soak the sponge in the bleach for 1 hour.
3. Pour the bleach solution down the sink.
4. Rinse clean.

HOW IT WORKS

The bleach solution kills the bacteria in the sponge. According to a 2015 test conducted by the Good Housekeeping Institute in conjunction with EMSL Analytical testing laboratory in Westmont, New Jersey, the bleach solution kills 99.9 percent of salmonella, *E. coli*, and pseudomonas in prepared test sponges (both scrub and cellulose).

SOAK IT UP

Other ways to disinfect a sponge:

- Saturate the sponge with water, and then heat it in a microwave oven (1 minute for a scrub sponge, 2 minutes for a cellulose sponge).
- Run the sponge through the dishwasher with your regular load of dishes and use the "heated dry" setting, which adds heat to promote drying.
- Mix ½ cup of white vinegar, 3 tablespoons of salt, and 1 cup of boiling water in a bowl. Soak the sponge overnight in the solution, and in the morning, rinse it clean.

Acknowledgments

At Chicago Review Press, I am grateful to my editor, Jerome Pohlen, for sharing my enthusiasm for this book and my entire Last-Minute series of books. I am also deeply thankful to project editor Lindsey Schauer; designer Jonathan Hahn; my agent, Laurie Abkemeier; researcher and photographer Debbie Green; photographer and model Julia Green; author Bob Blumer; author Carolyn Wyman; and my manager, Barb North. Above all, all my love to Debbie, Ashley, and Julia.

Bibliography

Alternative Cures: The Most Effective Natural Home Remedies for 160 Health Problems by Bill Gottlieb. Emmaus, PA: Rodale, 2000.

Another Use For by Vicki Lansky. Deephaven, MN: Book Peddlers, 1991.

Baking Soda Bonanza by Peter A. Ciullo. New York: Harper Perennial, 1995.

Bottom Line's Best-Ever Kitchen Hints by Joan Wilen and Lydia Wilen. Stamford, CT: Bottom Line, 2008.

"A Comparative Study to Evaluate the Effect of Honey Dressing and Silver Sulfadiazene Dressing on Wound Healing in Burn Patients" by P. S. Baghel, S. Shukla, R. K. Mathur, and R. Randa. *India Journal of Plastic Surgery* 42, no. 2 (July–December 2009): 176–81.

The Doctors Book of Home Remedies: Quick Fixes, Clever Techniques, and Uncommon Cures to Get You Feeling Better Faster by the Editors of Prevention. Emmaus, PA: Rodale, 2009.

Earl Proulx's Yankee Home Hints by Earl Proulx and the editors of *Yankee* magazine. Dublin, NH: Yankee, 1993.

"Efficacy of Cranberry Juice on *Helicobacter Pylori* Infection: A Double-Blind, Randomized Placebo-Controlled Trial" by L. Shang, J. Ma, K. Pan, et al. *Helicobacter* 10, no. 2 (April 2005): 139–45.

Encyclopedia of Household Hints and Dollar Stretchers by Michael Gore. New York: Doubleday, 1957.

Favorite Helpful Household Hints by the Editors of *Consumer Guide*. Skokie, IL: Publications International, 1986.

"Favourable Impact of Low-Calorie Cranberry Juice Consumption on Plasma HDL-Cholesterol Concentrations in Men" by Guillaume Ruel, Sonia Pomerleau, Patrick Couture, et al. *British Journal of Nutrition* 96 (2006): 357–64.

The Good Housekeeping Cookbook: 1,309 Recipes from America's Favorite Test Kitchen by Susan Westmoreland and edited by Good Housekeeping. New York: Hearst Books, 2007.

"A High Molecular Mass Constituent of Cranberry Juice Inhibits *Helicobacter Pylori* Adhesion to Human Gastric Mucus" by Ora Burger, Itzhak Ofek, Mina Tabak, et al. *FEMS Immunology and Medical Microbiology* 29 (2000): 295–301.

How to Break an Egg: 1,453 Kitchen Tips, Food Fixes, Emergency Substitutions, and Handy Techniques by the Editors of *Fine Cooking* magazine. Newtown, CT: Taunton Press, 2005.

"Inhibiting Interspecies Coaggregation of Plaque Bacteria with a Cranberry Juice Constituent" by E. I. Weise, R. Lev-Dor, Y. Kashamn, et al. *Journal of the American Dental Association* 129, no. 12 (December 1998): 1719–23.

In the Kitchen with Heloise by Heloise. New York: Perigee, 2000.

Joy of Cooking by Irma von Starkloff Rombauer and Marion Rombauer Becker. New York: Scribner, 1975.

Kitchen Cures: Homemade Remedies for Your Health by the Editors of *Reader's Digest*. New York: Reader's Digest Association, 2001.

Kitchen Hacks: How Clever Cooks Get Things Done by America's Test Kitchen. Brookline, MA: Cooks Illustrated, 2015.

Kitchen Hints from Heloise by Heloise. Emmaus, PA: Rodale, 2005.

Kitchen Wisdom by Frieda Arkin. New York: Consumers Union, 1977.

Mary Ellen's Best of Helpful Kitchen Hints by Mary Ellen Pinkham. New York: Warner Books, 1980.

Mary Ellen's Greatest Hints by Mary Ellen Pinkham. New York: Fawcett Crest, 1990.

1,628 Country Shortcuts from 1,628 Country People by the Editors of *Country* and *Country Woman* magazines. Greendale, WI: Reiman, 1996.

"One Way to Fight Food Waste: Revive Wilted Produce" by Carol Blymire. *Washington Post*, September 17, 2013.

Practical Problem Solver by *Reader's Digest*. Pleasantville, NY: Reader's Digest Association, 1991.

Re/Uses: 2,133 Ways to Recycle and Reuse the Things You Ordinarily Throw Away by Carolyn Jabs. New York: Crown, 1982.

Rodale's Book of Hints, Tips & Everyday Wisdom by Carol Hupping, Cheryl Winters Tetreau, and Roger B. Yepsen Jr. Emmaus, PA: Rodale, 1985.

Shameless Shortcuts by Fern Marshall Bradley and the Editors of *Yankee* magazine. Dublin, NH: Yankee, 2004.

Shoes in the Freezer, Beer in the Flower Bed by Joan Wilen and Lydia Wilen. New York: Fireside, 1997.

Solve It with Salt by Patty Moosbrugger. New York: Three Rivers Press, 1998.

Tips Cooks Love: Over 500 Tips, Techniques, and Shortcuts that Will Make You a Better Cook! by Sur La Table and Rick Rodgers. Kansas City, MO: Andrews McMeel, 2009.

Ultimate Camp Cookings by Mike Faverman and Pat Mac. Kansas City, MO: Andrews McMeel, 2011.

Vinegar, Duct Tape, Milk Jugs & More: 1,001 Ingenious Ways to Use Common Household Items to Repair, Restore, Revive, or Replace Just About Everything in Your Life by Earl Proulx and the editors of *Yankee* magazine. Emmaus, PA: Rodale, 1999.

What Einstein Told His Cook: Kitchen Science Explained by Robert L. Wolke with recipes by Marlene Parish. New York: Norton, 2010.

What Einstein Told His Cook 2: Further Adventures in Kitchen Science by Robert L. Wolke with recipes by Marlene Parish. New York: Norton, 2005.

Yankee Magazine's Practical Problem Solver by Earl Proulx and the editors of *Yankee* magazine. Dublin, NH: Yankee Books, 1998.

Yankee Magazine's Vinegar, Duct Tape, Milk Jugs & More by Earl Proulx and the editors of *Yankee* magazine. Dublin, NH: Yankee Books, 1999.

About the Author

Joey Green is the author of more than 60 books—including *Last-Minute Survival Secrets*, *Last-Minute Travel Secrets*, *Vacation on Location: Midwest*, and *The Electric Pickle*. A former contributing editor to *National Lampoon* and a former advertising copywriter at J. Walter Thompson, Joey has written television commercials for Burger King and Walt Disney World, and he won a Clio for a print ad he created for Eastman Kodak before launching his career as a best-selling author.

Joey has appeared on dozens of national television shows, including *The Tonight Show with Jay Leno*, *Good Morning America*, and *The View*. He has been profiled in the *New York Times*, *People*, the *Los Angeles Times*, the *Washington Post*, and *USA Today*, and he has been interviewed on hundreds of radio shows.

A native of Miami, Florida, and a graduate of Cornell University (where he founded the campus humor magazine, the *Cornell Lunatic*, still publishing to this very day), he lives in Los Angeles.